MIL RPWA 99

ROBERT PENN WARREN

—————— *A Study of the Short Fiction* ——

Twayne's Studies in Short Fiction

Gordon Weaver, General Editor
Oklahoma State University

Also available in Twayne's Studies in Short Fiction Series

ROBERT PENN WARREN

_____ *A Study of the Short Fiction* ___

Joseph R. Millichap
Western Kentucky University

TWAYNE PUBLISHERS • NEW YORK
Maxwell Macmillan Canada • Toronto
Maxwell Macmillan International • New York Oxford Singapore Sydney

Twayne's Studies in Short Fiction Series, No. 39

Copyright © 1992 by Twayne Publishers

Twayne Publishers
Macmillan Publishing Company
866 Third Avenue
New York, New York 10022

Maxwell Macmillan Canada, Inc.
1200 Eglinton Avenue East
Suite 200
Don Mills, Ontario M3C 3N1

Macmillan Publishing Company is part of the Maxwell Communication Group of Companies.

Library of Congress Cataloging-in-Publication Data

Millichap, Joseph R.
    Robert Penn Warren : a study of the short fiction / Joseph R. Millichap.
        p.   cm.—(Twayne's studies in short fiction ; no. 39)
    Includes bibliographical references and index.
    ISBN 0-8057-8346-6
    1. Warren, Robert Penn, 1905–   —Criticism and interpretation.
    2. Short story.   I. Title.   II. Series.
    PS3545.A748Z79   1992
    813'.52—dc20
                                                                    92-14380
                                                                    CIP

10 9 8 7 6 5 4 3 2 1

Printed in the United States of America

For Pat Bradley,
my friend across Warren Country,
who helped me in more ways than she knows or I can acknowledge.

Contents

Preface

Robert Penn Warren (1905–89) was modern America's greatest man of letters, a prolific and successful writer in several literary genres. Best known by the public for his novels, notably *All the King's Men* (1946), Warren himself believed lyric poetry was his major strength, while academic readers have been widely influenced by his literary and cultural criticism. In comparison with his voluminous production in other literary genres, Warren's short fiction proves relatively small in quantity—a single collection of 14 pieces. However, the overall quality of *The Circus in the Attic and Other Stories* (1947), as well as its connections to Warren's other writing, justifies closer critical attention than it has received. The relationship between the short fiction and Warren's accomplishments in other genres makes the relative accessibility of the stories and novellas particularly useful as an introduction to his total literary achievement. In fact, Warren's single short-fiction collection centers his canon in terms of genre and mode, as well as chronology. Most importantly, Warren's short fiction demonstrates his commitment to the romance of southern history, the central energizing theme of his long and productive literary career.

Given the quality, accessibility, and centrality of his short fiction, particularly in terms of his pervasive romance of southern history, Robert Penn Warren has been somewhat neglected as a short fictionist. General commentaries are often perfunctory or negative, while specific analyses have been restricted to his few well-known examples in this genre, notably "Blackberry Winter" (1946). The present study provides the book-length critique necessary for a thorough assessment of Warren's short fiction. As with other works in this series, *Robert Penn Warren: A Study of the Short Fiction* is divided into three major parts. Part 1 introduces Robert Penn Warren and the myth of southern history, considers the place of his short fiction in his overall literary achievement, and analyzes his single story collection as a short-fiction cycle. Part 2 presents a selection of Warren's own remarks on his short fiction and those of others drawn from interviews and his own critical writing. Part 3 offers a contrastive analysis, interpretation, and evaluation of the short fiction from two important Warren critics. In all, these three parts are intended as a critical introduction and overview for both the new and experienced reader of Robert Penn Warren and his short fiction.

In addition to the Warren scholars and critics acknowledged in the text, notes, and bibliography below, many people have provided assistance in the composition of *Robert Penn Warren: A Study of the Short Fiction*. Gordon Weaver, a fine short fictionist himself as well as general editor of this series, encouraged and supported this particular project; Twayne editor Liz Fowler also provided able assistance. Administrators at Western Kentucky University, including Dean Ward Hellstrom, Vice-President Robert Haynes, and President Thomas Meredith supported the project with research funds and released time. Colleagues at Western who listened to my ideas or read parts of my manuscript include Nancy Davis, Jim Flynn, Will Fridy, Joe Glaser, Mary Ellen Miller, and Joe Survant. My students at Western Kentucky University, particularly those in my American Short Fiction and Southern Renaissance seminars, gave lively response to many of the ideas developed in those classes and refined in the present study. My secretary, Earlene Cantrell, did yeoman work creating a typescript from my manuscript. Finally, my friend Pat Bradley provided careful editing and proofreading. Of course, all of my colleagues, friends, and family provided the sort of ineffable, yet vital, support so necessary for an endeavor of this sort.

Acknowledgments

I am grateful to the following individuals and institutions:

To the editors of *Studies in the Novel* and North Texas University for permission to reprint excerpts from Richard B. Sale's "An Interview in New Haven with Robert Penn Warren," 11 (Fall 1970): 325–54. Copyright© 1970, by North Texas State University.

To the editors of *Mississippi Quarterly* for permission to reprint Allen G. Shepherd's "Prototype, Byblow and Reconception: Notes on the Relation of Warren's *The Circus in the Attic* to His Novels and Poetry," 33 (Winter 1979–80): 3–17.

To the editors of *Mississippi Quarterly* for permission to reprint Randolph Runyon's "The View from the Attic: Robert Penn Warren's *Circus* Stories," 38 (Spring 1985): 119–35.

To Prentice Hall, Inc., for permission to reprint Robert Penn Warren's "Blackberry Winter: A Recollection," from Cleanth Brooks and Robert Penn Warren, eds., *Understanding Fiction*, 3rd ed. (Englewood Cliffs, N.J.: Prentice Hall, 1979). Copyright© 1979, by Prentice Hall, Inc.

To Silver, Burdett, and Ginn, Inc., for permission to reprint Robert Penn Warren's "On 'The Patented Gate and the Mean Hamburger,'" from William W. West, ed., *On Writing, By Writers* (Boston: Ginn and Company, 1966). Copyright© 1966, by Ginn and Company.

To the Warren Family and The Center For the Study of Robert Penn Warren for permission to use the frontispiece photograph.

Part 1

THE SHORT FICTION

Robert Penn Warren's "Twice-Told Tales"

Perhaps the salient feature of Robert Penn Warren's critical reputation in his place as modern America's leading man of letters. Only his most stalwart supporters would rank him among the very first of modern American novelists, or poets, or critics; however, his important work in all three genres ensures his singular place in the pantheon of modern American letters. His success is best demonstrated by his unique position as the only writer to win Pulitzer Prizes for both fiction (in 1947, for *All the King's Men*) and poetry (in 1957, for *Promises*, and again in 1979, for *Now and Then*). In corroboration with this public and popular acclaim, Warren remains the only recent writer to enjoy widespread critical recognition as both an important novelist and a major poet. Academic critics also value his nonfiction, notably his literary criticism, both theoretical and applied, as well as his works of biography, history, and cultural observation. Warren also produced interesting dramatic pieces, though in performance these seem more like closet dramas than not. The sum of Robert Penn Warren's efforts in all these genres proves significant not just to his literary reputation, but to a critical understanding of his literary achievement.

Working in the great romantic and realistic traditions of American letters, Warren produced a literary synthesis of genre, mode, idea, and style replicating the best of international modernism in general and its particular flowering in the Southern Renaissance. Warren's voluminous canon is a self-contained intertextuality informed by both the influences of traditional and modern writers and thinkers *and* by the interplay of his own creations in several genres and modes over several decades. As an intellectual much interested in philosophy and history, Warren enriches his works with a whole realm of ideas, producing in the process a powerful byplay of ideological abstractions and stylistic complexities. Dichotomies of genre or mode, theme or idea are often represented by contrasting styles that range from the intellectual and abstract to the colloquial and loquacious. Like the works of the most

3

important modern and contemporary writers, Warren's works admit a great complexity of elements, which in turn require a very careful critical approach allowing consideration of all of them.

At the same time, great writers embody in their works great themes, unifying principles that provide shape and meaning to their disparate efforts. As we would expect from the sheer size and complexity of Warren's canon, as well as its ambitious intentions and often brilliant successes, several universal themes emerge. Some of the most obvious examples articulated by Warren's critics include concern with the past, tradition, and history; the relationships of realism and romance, pragmatism and idealism, naturalism and supernaturalism; the tensions of fathers and sons, males and females, and whites and blacks in American culture. Of course, these themes create patterns of characterization and plot, setting and style in the individual works that are replicated throughout the Warren canon. As Warren himself commented, "every writer, no matter how great, has only one tale."[1] If we also consider the complex connections and contrasts of genre and mode in Warren's literary productions, a central theme energizes the work of modern America's greatest man of letters: the romance of southern history.

Robert Penn Warren described the South as the home-place of historical romance in a recent interview.

> The South is a special case. It lost the war and suffered hardship. That kind of defeat gives the past great importance. There is a need somehow to keep it alive, to justify it, and this works to transform the record of fact into legend. In the process, pain, dreariness, the particulars of the individual experience become absorbed in the romantic fable. The romance, you see, becomes stronger than the fact of any one story and changes it; even if you are only one or two generations removed from the event, it's hard to see through the romantic haze. (*Talking*, 72)

The events Warren considers here are the stuff of southern history, whether re-created in academic prose or in the folk poetry of "old tales and talking." His words "fable" and "story" also suggest that history and legend are, in turn, the stuff of southern literature, a narrative tradition steeped in romance and myth. Warren himself has always been haunted by his place and his past, while his critical and creative works often explore the complexities of romance as genre, frequently extending the term to his own creations in fiction and poetry. Warren's canon, the sum of all his narratives or his "one tale," becomes a romance of southern history, a creative dialectic between imagination and memory, fulfilling his own definition of the historical romance, by converting *"the past into a myth for the present."*[2]

Warren defined the historical romance in his brilliant introduction to the works of Nathaniel Hawthorne for the anthology *American Literature: The Makers and the Making* (1973). In his introduction Warren calls the historical romance Hawthorne's "shadowy territory," and "his own peculiar province," remarks perhaps as important for what they say about Warren's own work as for what they suggest about Hawthorne ("Hawthorne," 458). Warren transforms the regional history and romantic legend of his own peculiar province, the "Black Patch," or dark-fired tobacco country of western Kentucky and Tennessee, into historical romance rooted in the "shadowy territory" of both the American and the Southern Renaissance. Later he specifically applied the label of romance to his own novel *World Enough and Time*: "I was really thinking, I suppose, somewhere in the back of my mind about Hawthorne and some of his materials. It is a historical romance, but it's a philosophizing one—that's the difference. I have a modern man telling it and commenting on it as a modern man, you see. The modern man claims to have the documents—as I had some documents—and sees them in the modern way" (*Talking*, 261). This fascination with historical romance, extending over the century that separates *The Scarlet Letter* (1850) and *World Enough and Time* (1950), has been observed by many critics of American and southern literature, as well as critics of Warren's works.

In contrast, Warren's remarks about his own short fiction prove somewhat contradictory. The writer obviously was interested in the genre, as both his publishing practice and his critical comments indicate. His first published fiction was the novella "Prime Leaf," published in 1930; *Understanding Fiction* (1943), the second of the landmark textbooks compiled with Cleanth Brooks, was essentially a short-fiction anthology; and Warren not only wrote enough pieces for a short-fiction collection of his own, but made the effort to rewrite them, particularly the title novella, for *The Circus in the Attic and Other Stories* in 1947. His production in the genre is limited by comparison with the other genres of his canon, however, and he clearly stopped writing short fiction as such relatively early in his career.

In several places Warren indicates that he only writes short fiction as a means to earn money, and that materials that would have become poems were "used up" in short stories. Seemingly, when he no longer needed the money he stopped writing stories and gave himself over to poetry. Yet this explanation seems a bit ingenuous, for in several other places Warren indicates his lifelong pleasure in reading and writing short fiction. Moreover, the hiatus of a decade in his production of short poetry saw no additional short fiction. And, during this same period, the writer seemed intent on making money by means of novels, nonfiction, and textbooks. In any case, as the critical maxim succinctly puts it, "Trust the tale, not the teller." Although Warren acknowledges only three or four of his short fictions as worthy of his efforts, a close reading demonstrates that almost all of them remain very interesting for a contemporary audience as stories. The short fiction, as individual works and as a totality, relates in both particular and general ways to Warren's work in other genres, providing an accessible introduction to Warren's prodigious achievements. Finally, his short fiction is high in quality, central to his canon, readily accessible to his reader, and unified in achievement, as the following analyses will demonstrate.

Contemporary critical formulations such as the new definitions of ideology and intertextuality are useful tools for revealing the quality, importance, and unity of Warren's short fiction. For example, recent neo-Marxist critics, such as Louis Althusser, or neohistoricists, such as Frederic Jameson, have demonstrated that ideology is more pervasive than "ideas" as such. For Althusser, ideology unifies all cultural manifestations at a subliminal level that can be brought into consciousness by critical analysis. For the neohistoricists, cultural narratives are all texts to be read. As Jameson has remarked, "History is not in any sense itself a text or master text, a narrative or master narrative, but . . . it is inaccessible to us except in textual or narrative form."[3] This emphasis on the multiplicity of texts, within a unity of meaning, interests intertextual critics such as Julia Kristeva, who see all cultural texts intersecting at several levels, modifying each other, and creating new texts in which we discover cultural meaning. In other words, when one text is brought into a new juxtaposition with another text, its meaning changes and develops; an intertextuality occurs.

As noted above, Warren's ideology involves the romance of southern history, and thus his intertextuality contrasts history and romance. In all his individual works he constantly compares southern culture with its own romantic myths, often enough in terms of comparable texts. For example, in the novella that provides the title for his short-fiction collection, Warren juxtaposes Bolton Lovehart's stillborn history of Carruthers County with his colorful re-creations of the circus world. Both are "texts" that romanticize southern history, particularly Civil War history, so that Warren's narrative contrasts the reality of history with its romanticized image, a most significant intertextuality.

More importantly, the juxtaposition of Bolton's circus with the "other stories" of the title creates an intertextual unity in Warren's collection of short fiction itself. The overall theme of the romance of southern history, metaphorically represented by the image of the circus in the attic, or imagination transforming memory, pervades the volume, as it does Warren's whole canon. For example, the theme of initiation is present in several of Warren's stories, particularly in the cluster of three that follow the title novella—"Blackberry Winter," "When the Light Gets Green," and "Christmas Gift"—and also in "A Christian Education," "Testament of Flood," and "Prime Leaf." All the male initiates in these stories coalesce in an adamic figure, archetypal in some senses and biographical in others, reminiscent of earlier American innocents such as Anderson's George Willard, Hemingway's Nick Adams, or Steinbeck's Jody Tiflin.

This comparison of characters suggests other unities as well, for these adamic characters appear in unified story sequences, such as Anderson's *Winesburg, Ohio* (1919), Hemingway's *In Our Time* (1925), and Steinbeck's *The Red Pony* (1945). Contemporary criticism has come to recognize unified story sequences somewhere in the continuum between the anthology of discrete short stories and the totally unified novel. Several terms have been used to describe such works where the parts may stand alone or together, but critical practice seems to have settled on the "short-fiction cycle."[4]

This compound genre admits to analysis of elements found in both the shorter and longer works of fiction that inform it: character, plot, setting, style, and theme. Of course, the emphases are somewhat different in the short-fiction cycle. Characters are more often composites; plots are more fragmented; settings are more separated; style and theme are more varied and contrastive. We might speculate that these characteristics are more suited to modern life with its essential isolation, fragmentation, and rapid change. Certainly, the genre seems to have proliferated in the modern period both in America and in other cultures.

Robert Penn Warren's *The Circus in the Attic and Other Stories* should be viewed as just such a short-fiction cycle. Although its parts were

7

composed separately over a period from 1930 to 1946, they were arranged and integrated for the publication of the volume in 1947. As Warren's note at the beginning of the book indicates, his order is not chronological, neither in terms of compositional order nor of narrative sequence. Rather, he seems to use the novellas as framing pieces to give larger perspectives to the whole volume and to cluster the stories around topical or thematic motifs. As late as the reading of the galley proofs, Warren was tinkering with the order of the stories, transposing "Christmas Gift" and "Blackberry Winter" as well as "Her Own People" and "A Christian Education." It also proves significant that Warren revised the pieces from their earlier published versions, particularly the title novella. Although most of the changes were small, the enlarged historical framework in the opening piece provides thematic background for the entire volume. Therefore, all the pieces in *The Circus in the Attic and Other Stories* can be considered, by analogy with Nathaniel Hawthorne, Warren's "twice-told tales." This analogy proves apt not just in terms of composition—the reworking of separate texts into a new textuality—but also in terms of the romantic, archetypal, and mythic elements implied by the term "tale" as opposed to the term "short story."

The romance of southern history is the major unifying theme of the entire collection, but other themes are present in the several individual works. Initiation has been mentioned, along with memory and imagination, and by extension art, religion, and communication (or its failure). Although the pieces present a great variety of characters, the central figures are almost exclusively southern males at various stages of development from childhood to old age. The important events in their lives become parallel elements of plot: initiation, isolation, failure, frustration, and death. The settings are for the most part the towns and the country of Warren's "Black Patch" in western Kentucky and Tennessee. Style shows the range of Warren's efforts in other genres from first to third person, and from poetic or philosophical narration to tall-tale telling. In all, the pieces of Warren's collection can each stand alone, but standing together the whole becomes more than the sum of the parts. The individual works cohere in patterns that enrich each other, creating in the process one of Warren's most interesting and important books.

"The Circus in the Attic"

Although the relationship of Warren's novella to the volume it introduces proves important, "The Circus in the Attic" deserves critical consideration in its own right. Unfortunately, earlier criticism has for the most part ignored it, or slighted it in terms of presumed thematic confusions or structural defects.[5] A careful reading discovers the major structuring device of "The Circus in the Attic" to be the fictional psychobiography of Bolton Lovehart, which comes to represent the fictional history of Bardsville, Tennessee, and by extension the romance of southern history. The protagonist's major connection is symbolized by his arresting name, just as the significant name of the town symbolizes Bolton's relation to it as artist manqué.

Like many southern boys, young Lovehart bears his mother's patronymic as a first or middle name, symbolizing the linking of two prominent families. It also symbolizes the darker aspects of this union and the effect on the boy born from it. His mother's "passion for . . . the name of Bolton" is extended to her sickly son, assuaging her "disappointment in the marriage bed."[6] His mother's excessive love determines young Bolton's development, as if he were "a clever puppet," (*Circus*, 16), an interesting image suggesting the figures he later carves for his circus. His father, Simon Lovehart, passive after the shock of an emasculating Civil War wound, loves the boy, but from a discreet distance.

The narrator pauses twice to define the symbolic halves of Bolton's patronymic: love and heart. We are told love is not the proper name for his mother's egotistical feeling, but it will do because it "has been applied to other passions equally dark and deep" (*Circus*, 16). Later the Loveharts' family physician tells Bolton, "a heart is right in the middle of a man, or a woman for that matter, and in a manner of speaking it is them themselves" (*Circus*, 32). This dialogue takes place when the family doctor tries to tell Bolton that his mother is feigning "heart trouble" to thwart her son's marriage. In a revealing metaphor, Mrs. Lovehart compares both her heart and her son to a kitten she killed in her girlhood after it "betrayed" her by giving her a vicious scratch. Her

9

symbolically "bad" heart defines her selfhood as she incestuously clings to her son, in essence putting a "bolt on" his heart or selfhood. Later, as he carves his circus, he hides from his mother by working only late at night and "behind the always bolted door" (*Circus*, 41).

Once we recognize the ordering principle provided by this almost textbook case study of the Freudian "family romance," it becomes much easier to relate the seemingly disparate texts of the novella, including the historical preface and coda. Freud defines the "family romance" in his introduction to Otto Rank's *The Myth of the Birth of the Hero* (1909, 1914). An extremely suggestive study in its own right, Rank's thesis connects the hero myths of widely dispersed cultures through their shared narrative elements, in particular, the obscure or common backgrounds of protagonists later revealed to be of noble, or even divine, origin. In turn, Freud's introduction relates these myths to the stage of individual development wherein parental authority is displaced. A natural part of this process, Freud hypothesizes, consists of fantasies that replace the individual's real parents with better models in term of the individual's personal development. In a sense, Freud seems to posit the fantasies of neurotics who do not displace parental authority as the stuff of romance in the cultural sense, a complex of romanticized myths that are manifested in multiform cultural ideologies or texts.

The connection of Freud's Ur-Romance with the romance of southern history proves a fascinating exercise, one begun by a recent study. Richard King's excellent book, *A Southern Renaissance*, establishes the importance of family and family myth to both the Old and the New South and then demonstrates the traumatic effect of slavery, secession, defeat, Reconstruction, and segregation on the cultural maturation of the South. Southern myths and ideologies, in both their popular and literary manifestations, are in a Freudian sense the family romances of a neurotic culture. Following Freud's provocative suggestions, King places his central emphasis on Faulkner, though he also considers Robert Penn Warren's *All the King's Men*. A similar reading can be given to "The Circus in the Attic," which was finished directly after Warren's most famous novel; indeed, both works seem almost consciously ordered by these formulations.

As Warren's title novella develops by way of an historical introduction, we meet Bolton Lovehart through the parents who provide him his names.[7] All three are described closely and carefully, as in a historical tableau: "As we look back on them down the sixty years, they scarcely seem to move at all, to be fixed there in a photograph in an album to prove something sweet and sure about the past" (*Circus*, 17). It is as if they never change despite all the complex action of the novella. These symbolic relationships will remain fixed, caught in "a powerful, vibrating, multitudinous web of life" (*Circus*, 17), much like the one that Jack Burden discovers in the history of Cass Mastern that centers *All the King's Men*.

Bolton Lovehart is a good child, orderly and studious, storing his boyhood treasures, including his collection of arrowheads now bloodless with time and his father's regimental flag now faded with history, in the big attic room that will later house his circus. Then, just before his 12th birthday he begins his pattern of subconscious rebellion against the determinations of his parents. Without any consideration, he wanders into a fundamentalist meeting on Cadman's Creek and allows himself to be baptized by total immersion. This rejection of his parents' genteel Episcopalianism—both his father and his maternal grandfather were "High Church" clergymen—is described with sexual undertones and circus motifs. The tall preacher's black coat glittered with "a few gold willow leaves . . . like spangles," while the dress of a young initiate billowed "about her like a dancer" (*Circus*, 21). As she struggles to pull her dress down, the girl grasps the preacher's hand to her breast, "arching her back somewhat, in surrender" (*Circus*, 21). The connection with Freud is interesting, for he suggests that at puberty the nature of the family romance changes to fantasies that specifically supplant the father; at the same time, Rank's analysis of the Christ myth also proves instructive, as Christ's baptism by his cousin John preceded his public mission.

When he is 16, Bolton commits the ultimate "bad boy" act; he "bolts on," running off with the circus. He sees it as "a flame-streaked Dionysiac reveling" (*Circus*, 24), and again his fascination with the "savage, symbolic beasts" of this "barbarous tribe" (*Circus*, 24) seems pointedly sexual as he faces the stresses of puberty. Of course, he is eventually overtaken and returned to the dull routine of Professor Darter's Academy, from which he ultimately graduates as valedictorian. Yet his rebellion against this genteel education by a surrogate father is underlined by Bolton's assumption of a false name, and a rather common one at that, Joe Randall. The suggestions of the name perhaps extend even further in terms of another surrogate father, Joseph of Bethlehem.

At this point of maturation, as Bolton plans to attend the Episcopal

11

University of the South at Sewanee, his father suddenly dies of a stroke. He should be ready to go off and be his own man, but Bolton must stay home with his mother for the year. And when he goes away to college the next year, his mother feigns the first of her "heart attacks." Again he stays home as dutiful son and surrogate lover, teaching at the Darter Academy and researching a history of Carruthers County. After four years he has a romantic love affair with Sara Darter, "the old professor's daughter." In a battle of sexual wills worthy of D. H. Lawrence, Mrs. Lovehart keeps her son as her "lover," while Sara flees to the larger world of Nashville after coldly seducing and abandoning the bewildered Bolton.

From this juncture, Bolton's acts of rebellion become ever more circumspect, ever more inward, ever more imaginative. He takes a job working as the "impresario" of Bardsville's first picture-show in 1913, another world of the imagination where on the silver screen he views gladiatorial scenes from *Ben Hur* or "some dark-haired full-busted beauty in black dress, gorgeous with jewels and fringes" (*Circus*, 38). His mother again intervenes; to work at the picture-show would sully the names of both the Boltons and the Loveharts. Thus, he returns to his history, to be supported by his mother's rental properties in "nigger town." Bolton Lovehart has reached the christologic age of 33 and he has completed only one chapter in his book, ironically named "The Coming of the Fathers," which chronicles the period of Bardsville's founding.

Now Bolton finds his real work. "That Winter, just after Christmas, he begins to make the circus" (*Circus*, 40). A toy circus in a store's window display gives him the first impulse. He carves a tiger, then a lion, next an elephant, a ringmaster, and finally his masterpiece, "the girl acrobat with blue eyes and a skirt of silk" (*Circus*, 41). Once again, he feels the "old excitement he had felt that night, years back . . . when he watched the flame-streaked hoarse tumult as the circus was loaded" (*Circus*, 41). Of course, the circus becomes more than a personal symbol; its context here makes it universal, a symbol of an imaginative, creative, and romantic vision of life, where it recalls the central symbols of Hawthorne's tales and romances of art and artists. An almost metaphysical image links his history book and his circus art as texts. Bolton tells his mother he needs the paints he uses to decorate his figures to make a map of Carruthers County. Of course, his circus becomes a map of his own imagination, a creative vision of his own *patria* or fatherland.

World War I means almost nothing for the young historian, perhaps because he is immersed both in his historical research for a chapter on the Civil War and in the expansion of his private circus. Only with the news of the Armistice does he come forth from the attic into the circuslike "tumult," to see the bonfire and hear the shouting and singing, at the foot of the Confederate monument in front of the court house," (*Circus*, 43). But he quickly returns home to "his victory" (*Circus*, 43), kissing his mother and ascending into the attic.

This psychological symbolism is even better demonstrated after his mother's death, from her first actual heart attack, in 1934. Our narrator comments: "The reason for his occupation was gone. The old pleasure was gone, the compulsion. There was no need to lie anymore" (*Circus*, 46). Bolton Lovehart can live in the real world now, but at 54 he finds it hard to enter. He has lived too long in his family romance. His mother's money and his father's church sustain him until he meets the social-climbing Widow Parton. They marry in 1939, and she begins to plan the restoration of the Lovehart home to her tastes.

When the Second World War arrives, Bolton's happiness is complete. At last he has a purpose in real life as well as in his imagination. He becomes the hero of the home front: lecturing on military strategies, organizing paper and scrap drives, and entertaining the trainees from the nearby army camp. His wife's college-age son, Jasper, returns home an officer, but disappoints his mother by marrying Janie Murphy, "a Roman Catholic to boot" (*Circus*, 49). In a reprise of the earlier battles of sexual wills, the cocky Jasper wins easily, slapping his mother on the rump, calling her "Old Girl," and then bolting off into the big world. Of course, it is the same world Jack Burden faced at the end of *All the King's Men*, a world at war. In 1943 Jasper Parton dies a hero's death in the Italian campaign, winning the Congressional Medal of Honor.

After his first shock, Bolton Lovehart realizes his "great idea." He donates his circus to a children's bazaar at the Episcopal church. The death of his surrogate son, which recalls his own psychic death years earlier, brings his circus out into the world to live. Sold piece by piece, it delights dozens of children and raises $200 for the Red Cross. Bolton's photograph is printed in the newspaper beside his "lost" circus, an interesting juxtaposition of texts. At a memorial service for Jasper, Bolton presents another text, an inspired speech that confirms his symbolic fatherhood. Before he stops, choked by his own feelings, he declares that all the young men overseas are like his sons.[8]

But if Bolton has truly become a father, he was never really a lover.

13

As the war effort moves toward victory, and the home front celebrates, his wife is killed in a bloody highway accident. She had been joyriding with Captain Cartwright, an officer from the base; both had been drinking, and the Bardsville gossips suspect more. Bolton Lovehart is crushed; with the end of the war, he returns to the point where we met him at the outset. He is at home with his tools and paints, re-creating the circus in the attic:

> The last victories came. The last blood was shed in the ruined streets of Berlin. Half the world away, American fleets lifted some dream island in the morning light and the bombardment began, while landing craft skeetered crazily shoreward. People in Bardsville knew how it was. They could see it in the newsreel after the feature. Then the bomb fell on Hiroshima.
>
> It meant nothing, however, to Bolton Lovehart. For some time now, all day long and far into the night, he had sat in the attic, leaning over his table, where lay the block of soft pine, the glue pot, the wire, the awl, the knife, the paint tubes and brushes, the bits of cloth and needles and scissors. Finally he had found his way back. (*Circus*, 60)

This passage of two paragraphs, set off as its own section in the text, marks an interesting metaphoric crux. Once again the nightmares of history become the dream worlds of the circus. The newsreel, an entertainment posing as documentary, recalls Bolton's brief movie career during the previous war. However, like the war of 1917–18, the apocalypse of 1945 means nothing to Lovehart, for he is busy re-creating history as romance. He has found his way back, as the narrator tells us, to his historical text.

Bardsville becomes a Vanity Fair of postwar prosperity. Yet this image of the inauthentic, corrupted future, suggesting the concluding coda of *World Enough and Time*, does not end the novella. Rather, the last paragraph takes us back to the circus in the attic. Janie Murphy Parton has married a foreman from the furniture factory, and she is letting go of Jasper's memory. But he will not be lost in the welter of history:

> He will go away where he belongs, to join the circus in the attic. He will join Seth Sykes and drunken Cash Perkins and all the heroes who ever died for all their good reasons, and old Lem Lovehart, who laid himself down amid birdsong at dusk and was scalped by a

Chicasaw, and Simon Lovehart with the wound and the prayer book
as his truth, and Louise Bolton Lovehart with her dear, treacherous
heart in her bosom, and the kitten little Louise Bolton flung from
her window to thud on the paving bricks, and the bloodless
arrowheads and the fading flag of Simon Lovehart's regiment, and
the song, "Let the nearer waters roll," which they sang at the
baptizing and the song they sang in the square the night of the
armistice in 1918, and the painted animals carved from wood and the
sinister ring master and the girl acrobat with the frivolous skirt and
round blue painted eyes, and all the things by which Bardsville had
lived, and found life worth living, and died. And Jasper will be at
home there. (*Circus*, 61–62).

In other words, memory is subsumed in imagination, and art
becomes myth, the end product of history. Finally, "The Circus in the
Attic" is a *Kunstlerroman*, the psychobiography of an artist. Bolton
Lovehart's book was stillborn; his eulogy for Jasper abortive; his movie
career unsuccessful. But his circus comes alive in the teeming images
of memory. For Warren's vision of history is a circus. The Battle of
Bardsville, Bolton's baptism, Bardsville's picture show, its Armistice
night, "nigger town," the home front, and newsreels of the Second
World War—all are described in vivid circus imagery.

Viewed by the cold eye of history, the carved circus is the pathetic
play world of an arrested adolescent, but in the creative vision of
romance it projects the truth of imagination, like poetry, "the little
myth we make" out of history, "the big myth we live." It seems that
something of Warren's definition of poetry finds its way into the
description of Bolton's obsession: "When he finished some new
creature to add to the little throng which cluttered the shelves and
floor, or devised some new apparatus for the circus, he felt for one
moment, up there above the world, the peace and purity of spirit that
comes when vision and cunning are commensurate" (*Circus*, 42). We
might do well to compare another menagerie, one of glass created a few
years earlier in 1943 by the southern playwright Tennessee Williams in
his best-known drama, a menagerie that represents all the possibilities
of the imagination.

So if Bolton Lovehart ever lives at all it is through the circus in the
attic, just as our narrator lives through the imaginative carnival of the
tale, and just as our author lives in the creation of the mythic menagerie
of his short-fiction collection. For Bolton Lovehart is in some sense a

projection of Warren himself, of what he might have been if his somewhat domineering mother had kept him home to be the poet laureate of Todd County, Kentucky. Warren left to become an international literary artist, and from his memory his imagination carved the sinister stranger of "Blackberry Winter," the seductive schoolgirl of "Testament of Flood," the heroic/pathetic grandfathers of "When the Light Gets Green" and "Prime Leaf." Throughout the canon other incarnations of these figures appear in titles like *Meet Me in the Green Glen, At Heaven's Gate*, and *Night Rider*, or in a half-dozen other novels, or in dozens of memorable poems, or even in numerous volumes of history and criticism. As I indicated at the outset, Robert Penn Warren is a southern Renaissance man. He is such precisely because he has narrated for all of us the romance of southern history, creating out of his "own peculiar province" the universal life and truth of art.

"And Other Stories"

"Blackberry Winter"

Perhaps no single, postwar American story has been so often antholo-
gized, so frequently alluded to, or so highly praised as "Blackberry
Winter."[9] Warren himself acknowledged its special importance by
including it in the second edition of *Understanding Fiction* (1959) along
with his introductory essay, "'Blackberry Winter': A Recollection."
The last story he wrote, in the fall and winter of 1945–46, it is not only
his best known but his best effort in the genre. Obviously "Blackberry
Winter" stands successfully on its own; indeed, it was first published as
a separate chapbook by the Cummington Press in 1946. But it is best
read and most fully understood within the full context of Warren's
short-fiction cycle, *The Circus in the Attic and Other Stories*.

Warren placed his finest story second in the volume directly after the
introductory novella, whose title has metaphoric and thematic impli-
cations that provide a key to understanding this story. The story is a
work of recollection on the parts of both author and narrator, a blending
of memory and imagination, of history and romance. The story's own
symbolic title, "Blackberry Winter," suggests its romantic themes and
images. Warren's most famous tale does not depend on poetic prose or
narrative artifice; rather, it balances a precise realism of detail,
including accurate social observation and a harsh naturalism of theme
against its lyric recollection of youthful innocence. Warren connects the
story with the two major works he had just completed: his finest novel
All the King's Men and his important introduction to Coleridge's "The
Ancient Mariner." "Blackberry Winter" can be seen in tension between these two poles of realistic and naturalistic fiction, on the one
hand, and romantic and lyric poetry, on the other. And, in these
dichotomies of genre and mode, he establishes his major structuring
device: the contrasting of opposites in terms of characters, events,
settings, and themes.

The author's introductory essay (reprinted in Part 2) warns the reader
that the story's realism does not derive from autobiographical experience; in his recollection, the writer insists that he did not know these
people and that no tramp ever threatened him. He did, however, know

17

this world, for it is clearly that of his boyhood in the Black Patch country of Kentucky and Tennessee. The lyrical impulse that creates the story is autobiographical; Warren recollected "the particular thread"[10] that led him back into the past as the boyhood desire to go barefoot in spring and summer. During a winter of personal and cultural discontent, the writer recalled this image of an idyllic personal and cultural past. Although he had finished his two major projects, he was anxious about their success and feeling the additional anxiety of his recent 40th birthday in the setting of "a big, modern, blizzard-bit" Minneapolis ("Recollection," 377). The larger culture also knew in that winter of 1945–46 the full horrors of the Holocaust and Hiroshima as well as the failure of the post war visions of peace and plenty. As with the composition of his first published fiction, "Prime Leaf," his farewell to short fiction, "Blackberry Winter," was a way of recapturing a life from which he had separated. In an interesting image he calls its effort a sort of "Indian summer," of his short fiction ("Recollection," 382).

In the midst of a dark cold winter, the writer recalled the youthful joy of summer vacation, of going barefoot—"a declaration of independence from the tyranny of winter and school and, even, your own family" ("Recollection," 640). This freedom symbolized a reentry into nature, into the woods and streams of the countryside around his grandfather's farm, as Warren puts it, "what the anthropologists call a rite of passage," ("Recollection," 640). But spring was often betrayed by a "cold spell," when a northern front would dip across the border country bringing a "gully-washer" of a storm and a return of winter's tyrannies. These unseasonal cold spells provide a mirror image of "Indian Summer" and likewise have a sequence of folk names derived from the blossoms scattered by these northern fronts: daffodil winter in April, dogwood winter in May, blackberry winter in June when the blackberry bushes are white with their delicate blossoms.

Warren opens his story with blackberry winter in the recollection of a narrator named Seth, then nine years old, circa 1910, in the border country of Tennessee. Standing on the kitchen hearth of his family's farmhouse, arguing with his mother about wearing shoes in summertime, and wondering if he dare sneak out barefoot, the consternation of the boy leads the adult narrator, 35 years later, to muse on the nature of time. To a boy, time is "a kind of climate in which things are," (*Circus*, 64); in other words, time is not movement." And if there is movement, the movement is not time itself, any more than a breeze is a climate" (*Circus*, 64). In other words, the boy does not understand how time changes things, how the orderly progression of time will lead to disorder and death. Of course, the destructive blasts of the storm demonstrate that nature as well as time will generate more than gentle breezes in life. The man knows the boy wants to be barefoot "and make the perfect mark of your foot . . . on the glistening auroral beach of the world" (*Circus*, 64).[11] In this innocent dawn of life the fixed, stable, orderly progression seems immutable, until the voice from the kitchen reiterates, "It's June . . . but it's blackberry winter" (*Circus*, 64).

At this juncture in his composition, Warren had his recollections, his nostalgia, "but something has to happen if there is to be more than a dreary lyric poem posing as a story" ("Recollection," 640). Indeed, themes and events of this story would be replayed in a half-dozen later poems, but in 1945–46 Warren was writing short fiction. His narrative inspiration has a sense of drama and of romance: "*Enter mysterious stranger*" ("Recollection," 640, emphasis Warren's). The writer's portentous announcement develops the archetypal aspect of the tramp who appears out of the woods near the river seeking odd jobs. A familiar character in tales by Hawthrone, Poe, and Melville, the mysterious stranger provides a title for Mark Twain's darkest story, as well as the protagonist for his cautionary tale of American nightmares, "The Man That Corrupted Hadleyburg." As Warren puts it in his recollection, "The tramp who has walked into my story had been waiting a long time in the wings of my imagination" ("Recollection," 640); undoubtedly, the mysterious stranger, so often connected in literature with the supernatural and the subconscious, is a part of the generic American imagination as well.

Warren goes on to recall "an image drawn, no doubt from a dozen unremembered episodes of childhood, a city bum turned country tramp . . . a dim image of what, in one perspective, our human condition is" ("Recollection," 640). So Warren's figure is no comedic, picturesque re-creation in the mode of Chaplin's Little Tramp, but the real thing, the human refuse produced by urban changes. His clothes and shoes are an outlandish combination of city and country; his features are gray and nondescript; his possessions no more than a parcel wrapped in newspaper and a switchblade knife, "the kind of mean knife just made for devilment and nothing else" (*Circus*, 67). The knife focuses Warren's description of his entry as the bum draws it against threatening dogs: "He just held the knife blade close against the right leg, low down, and kept on moving down the path" (*Circus*, 68). Mechanized, yet almost magical, deadly and somewhat phallic, the switchblade forms a perfect correlative for the tramp, a social yet symbolic outcast easily associated with the darker aspects of life—failure, loneliness, violence, compulsion, and death—and with the archetypes who represent them: the prodigal, the demon, the outcast, the grim reaper, the devil himself, the serpent in Eden.

The nameless tramp, in short, represents everything that the innocent narrator has yet to encounter in his ordered, stable life. The boy's mother is opposite to the tramp: clean, brisk, tanned, steady, self-reliant, and fearless. She seems so youthful and vital that the narrator still cannot reconcile himself to the fact that she has been dead these many years—here the reader realizes fully the author's intended play between past and present. The narrator knows many women would have been afraid of this stranger, but his mother meets him calmly, offering food in return for help in cleaning up the storm damage to her poultry coops and flower beds. Probably she intends an act of charity, for the jobs are paltry, mere boy's work, and the tramp seems disinclined to do any real labor. When Seth follows, watching him at his efforts with the dead chicks and wilted flowers, the tramp chases him off to find his father at the washed-out bridge near the farm.

An even more obvious foil for the forlorn stranger, the narrator's father is "a tall, limber man, who carried himself well" and sits his horse "quiet and straight" (*Circus*, 73). His cowhide boots, hunting coat, and clean pants, "made him look very military, like a picture" (*Circus*, 77). When his father lifts him to the pommel of his saddle for a better look at the flooded crossing, Seth enjoys a warm secure feeling in the midst of the strange crowd assembled to assess the damage of the flood. Many of them are "pore white trash" (*Circus*, 75), sharecroppers ruined by the unseasonable storm that has washed out their cash crop, the dark-fired tobacco. A grotesque drowned cow floats downstream to strike the bridge girders as if to punctuate the scene of natural disaster and untimely death. The cow belonged to one of the poor whites, Milt Alley, who with his "passel" of children is hardly better off than the urban tramp. When Seth asks his father if he thinks Milt Alley has another cow, his father replies quietly, "you say, 'Mr. Alley,'" indicating this thoughtful man's identification with his poor-white counterpart in this time of loss. This social parallelism is underscored when a poor-white boy not much older than Seth, "who might just as well as not have been the son of Milt Alley," (*Circus*, 76), embarrasses himself by speculating about eating "drown cow." A white-bearded man, a veteran of Nathan Bedford Forrest's long raids, summarizes the wisdom time provides: "Live long enough, he said, and a man will settle for what he can git" (*Circus*, 77). The old man with the white beard provides a connection with Seth's "military" father as well as an incarnation of the recurring nightmares of war and famine.

Warren then shifts the realistic focus of the story from dispossessed whites to exploited blacks, when the symbolic narrative moves from the old white man to an old black man. Old Jebb (whose name Warren tells us in his "Recollection" ironically recalls another gallant Confederate commander, J.E.B. Stuart) is "up in his seventies" but "he was strong as a bull" (*Circus*, 81), the patriarch of the small community of black tenants on the farm. Most of the black sharecroppers come and go, to be "shiftless somewhere else" (*Circus*, 78), the narrator says, perhaps echoing his father who "was always threatening to get shut of them" (*Circus*, 78). The adult narrator seems conscious of racial tensions and ironies when he contrasts Old Jebb and his common-law wife, Dellie, some 30 years younger than her husband, as "clean and clever Negroes . . . what they used to call 'white-folks' niggers'" (*Circus*, 77). Old Jebb and Dellie work hard in the father's fields and in their own garden, being especially "careful to keep everything nice around their cabin" (*Circus*, 77). They have a son, Little Jebb, about two years older than the narrator and his closest playmate.

Clearly, the black family mirrors the white family in a textbook illustration of the southern family romance posited by Richard King and others. Of Old Jebb, the narrator tells us, "He was a good man, and I loved him next to my mother and father" (*Circus*, 81). On other levels, Old Jebb is a surrogate father, or grandfather, with "the kindest and wisest old face in the world" (*Circus*, 81). He became the archetypal "wise old man" because he is part of the stable order of the farm, but at the same time separate from it—the "other" who can instruct the young initiate in the mysteries of time and change. He is also a foil for the tramp in the development of the narrator's consciousness: both are dark, enigmatic figures—one good, one bad. Within this configuration, Dellie can represent the shadow image of the mother, or of the female as other, while Little Jebb is the darker double of Seth himself.

Of course, the young Seth is unconscious of these parallels; he is only seeking the warmth of Dellie's hearth and Little Jebb's company after his cold barefoot walk from the creek. Even the adult narrator seems only generally aware of these connections and ironies as he retells his tale, though they do seem to emerge clearly in the final coda that sums up the history of the characters. The careful reader, of course, sees more in the story, especially in the context created by the short-fiction cycle. One symbol proves particularly arresting in comparison with the title novella. The young white boy asks his black friend if he can play with his train. "Old Jebb had put spool wheels on three cigar boxes and put wire links between the boxes to make a train for Jebb. The box that was the locomotive had the top closed and a length of broom stick for a smoke stack" (*Circus*, 80). Even within the story this homemade toy provides an important symbolic nexus. On the most basic level, it replicates the black family's careful, clever imitation of the white family, who could have bought a metal toy train for their son. At the cultural level, the train in 1910 would have been the primary symbol of mechanization, industrialization, and urbanization; in other short fictions, such as "Prime Leaf," it takes its realistic place as a primary agent of social and cultural change. Although no actual trains appear in this story, Old Jebb is said to look like "cast iron streaked with rust" (*Circus*, 81), while Dellie in her prime has the energy of "an old-fashioned black steam thrasher engine" (*Circus*, 79). Most interesting is the comparison with Bolton Loveheart's model circus, especially in the way the toy train becomes a text of sorts in which to read the relationships within the culture and the changes overtaking them.

The narrator's visit to the cabins emphasizes these same themes. As he approaches he contrasts Jebb and Dellie's cabin with the two others occupied by the constantly shifting poor black families, people little better off than the white tramp. Also, the storm has transformed the neat yard by washing all the trash out from under their raised cabin.

> I took a few steps up the path to the cabin, and then I saw that the drainage water had washed a lot of trash and filth out from under Dellie's house. Up toward the porch, the ground was not clean any more. Old pieces of rag, two or three rusted cans, pieces of rotten rope, some hunks of old dog dung, broken glass, old paper, and all sorts of things like that had washed out from under Dellie's house to foul her clean yard. It looked just as bad as the yards of the other cabins, or worse. It was worse, as a matter of fact, because it was a surprise. I had never thought of all that filth being under Dellie's house. It was not anything against Dellie that the stuff had been

under the cabin. Trash will get under any house. But I did not think
of that when I saw the foulness which had washed out on the ground
which Dellie sometimes used to sweep with a twig broom to make
nice and clean. (*Circus*, 78–79)

This paragraph is worth quoting at length because in his introduction
Warren points to it as the central image of the story. He then connects
this "homely" image with the larger social and cultural contexts of war
and peace. At the time he wrote "Blackberry Winter," he was reading
Herman Melville's Civil War poetry, notably the poem "Conflict of
Convictions," about the origins of the war:

> Whatever the rights and wrongs of the matter, the war, Melville
> said, would show "the slimed foundations" of the world. There was
> the sense in 1945, even with victory, that we had seen the slimed
> foundations, and as I now write this, the image that comes into my
> mind is the homely one from my story—the trash washed by the
> storm from under Dellie's cabin to foul her pridefully clean yard.
> And I should not be surprised if the picture in the story had its roots
> in the line from Melville as well as in such a fact, seen a hundred
> times in my rural boyhood. So the mixed feelings I had in our
> moment of victory in 1945, Melville's poem, and not only the image
> of Dellie's cabin, but something of the whole import of my little
> story, belong, it seems, in the same package. ("Recollection," 639)

The images of change continue, for Dellie is not her usual bustling
self but is sick in bed with what Old Jebb later identifies as "woman-
mizry" (*Circus*, 82). And when Little Jebb and the narrator get noisy
playing with the cigar-box train, Dellie slaps her son in an "awful" way
that brings the boy to silent tears. This behavior startles the narrator
almost as much as it would if his mother had slapped him in the same
fashion. The contrast of the two mother figures is reinforced when Old
Jebb connects Dellie's illness with "the change of life and time"
(*Circus*, 82), particularly with the change of seasons. When the white
boy tells his black mentor that his mother says it's only blackberry
winter, Old Jebb portentously replies, "too late for blackberry winter,
blackberries done bloomed" (*Circus*, 82). The grizzled patriarch connects this storm with the biblical flood and with the millennial end of
the earth itself. Their discussions conclude with Old Jebb's cryptic
warning as he watches the shoeless boy shiver with the cold, "you
ketch your death" (*Circus*, 83).

The narrator had told the blacks about the tramp, but had not told his father. A careful reader might wonder why; perhaps the excitement of the flood distracted the boy so that he simply forgot. Or possibly the author forgot himself, for the passage telling the blacks was added to the original manuscript. If the father were told, it would undoubtedly short-circuit the development of the story, for he would certainly have ridden directly home for the confrontation that concludes the story *after* young Seth has visited the black family.

The final confrontation works on both realistic and archetypal levels. The farmer, probably wanting to be rid of the "shiftless" tramp, dismisses him with a half dollar for a morning's work—the correct amount in 1910, the narrator notes. The tramp, possibly covering his own need and disappointment, replies, "I didn't want to work on your ———farm" (*Circus*, 89). Seth is astounded at the word, one "they would have frailed me to death for using" (*Circus*, 89). In Warren's typescript, he was more forthcoming; it reads "f——g farm." Evidently, the word was no more printable in 1946 than in 1910, though it is interesting to know Warren's intentions.

For the "f-word" raises a flurry of sexual connotations and not just for the nine-year-old Seth. In particular, it would have underlined even more markedly the tramp as a threat, even a sexual threat, to the prelapsarian innocence and order of farm and family life. The tramp asserts his oedipal threat by spitting at the father's "military" boots, and by fingering the switchblade knife in his pocket. Seth thought "that if that glob had hit my father's boot something would have happened" (*Circus*, 85). But doesn't, and under the father's steady gaze the tramp retreats without pulling his knife. He stops only for his newspaper parcel and then hightails it for the main road. Strangely, the boy Seth seems compelled to follow the stranger, staying a few feet away from him, asking "Where did you come from?" and "Where are you going?" (*Circus*, 85). The tramp replies only "you don't stop following me and I cut yore throat, you little son-of-a-bitch" (*Circus*, 86).

Warren does not end the story here with the boy watching the tramp disappear down the pike toward town. Instead he provides a coda in which the adult narrator, now 44, sums up the meaning of the incident as he sees it from the perspective of three and a half decades, from 1945, the same year in which Warren wrote the story. Of course, his parents are dead, both lost while he was still a boy. His father died of lockjaw, cut by "the blade of a mowing machine" (*Circus*, 86), as if the grim reaper had returned to mow him down. His self-reliant mother died of a broken heart after she sold the farm and moved to town. Dellie died too, though some years later. Old Jebb lived on, and was at least 100 when the narrator last saw him in town and on relief during the depression, still strong but lonely and old, like a lost patriarch. Little Jebb, the narrator's black double, grew up to be "mean and ficey," killing another black in a fight and still serving a term in the state penitentiary. The tramp he never saw again. But the narrator concludes his tale by noting "But I did follow him, all the years" (*Circus*, 87).

Warren's ambiguous final line has been given a number of readings by critics and scholars; however, he provides his own gloss in his recollection of the story's composition: "Had the boy then stopped or not? Yes, of course, literally, in the muddy lane. But at another level—no. Insofar as later he had grown up, had really learned something of the meaning of life, he had been bound to follow the tramp all his life, in the imaginative recognition, with all the responsibility which such a recognition entails, of this lost, mean, defeated, cowardly, worthless, bitter being as somehow a man" ("Recollection," 643). In other words, the tramp symbolizes, like the evil angel in Eden, the full knowledge of the fallen human condition, of the progression of time and the inevitability of change. The succeeding decades have proved that fathers fail, mothers die, sons turn prodigal, brother kills brother, the garden paradise is lost, the foundations slimed, and only the trash remains, the detritus of nature and culture. For our contemplation, however, we have the arresting tale from this "mariner" narrator who has lived through this fortunate fall, through depression and war, without losing his humanity or even his desire to understand it better. As Robert Penn Warren, the ultimate narrator, puts it in his recollection, "I wanted the story to give some notion that out of change and loss a human recognition may be redeemed, more precious for being no-longer innocent" ("Recollection," 642).

"When the Light Gets Green"

Warren probably clustered his strong initiation stories after "The Circus in the Attic" in terms of quality, centrality, and accessibility. "Blackberry Winter" is certainly his most successful story both in Warren's own view and by general critical agreement. His arrangement makes sense on a practical level by engaging the reader with very powerful works concerned with universal themes. At the same time, the initiation stories extend many of the themes first presented in the title novella, something of a long initiation tale itself, notably the romance of southern history. These initiation stories in some ways make these themes more accessible, as their first-person narrators comment on them rather directly. Therefore, "When the Light Gets Green" has been generally well received by reviewers and critics.[12]

"When the Light Gets Green," the third selection in Warren's short-fiction cycle, certainly fits this pattern. Probably his best-known and most critically considered story after "Blackberry Winter," "When the Light Gets Green" seems even more directly evocative of the romance of southern history, even as it is more complexly connected with Warren's personal life and literary career. Unlike "Blackberry Winter," about which Warren made a specific biographical disclaimer, "When the Light Gets Green" has a rather direct biographical background in Warren's close relationship with his maternal grandfather, Thomas Penn. The factual details of his grandfather Penn's life have been reiterated in Warren's prose (both in interviews and reminiscence) and in his later reminiscent poetry. "When the Light Gets Green" is, in a sense, recycled fiction as well, for it is reconstructed from a chapter of Warren's second unpublished novel, the completed but untitled work that is also the source of the stories "The Love of Elsie Barton: A Chronicle" and "Testament of Flood." Warren composed the untitled novel, according to his own note, "about 1933 and 1934 in Tennessee," while the original typescript of "When the Light Gets Green" bears the notation "1st Draft 1935." The story was first published in the *Southern Review* in 1936, and since has often been reprinted.

The parallels between the grandfather of this story and Warren's grandfather Penn are easily established by comparing the long biographical sketch of the fictional grandfather that centers the story and Warren's various factual reminiscences. Both the general biographical outline and the specific details and language prove very similar. Thomas Penn, like the grandfather of the story, was born in west Tennessee where he raced horses as a young man before the Civil War, later rode with Nathan Bedford Forrest during the war, and killed enemy "guerrillas" during the uneasy peace that followed. After the war grandfather Penn came to Kentucky to escape the revenge of a rival faction, where he was a tobacco farmer and, briefly, a tobacco broker, in rural Trigg County outside the small spa at Cerulean Springs. The young Robert Penn Warren spent his summers there, with his grandfather as a constant companion. The details of both factual and fictional grandfathers' age, appearance, conversation, recollection, and reading also match almost perfectly.[13]

In the later, reminiscent poems that center on his grandfather, such as "When Life Begins," "Old Time Childhood in Kentucky," "Court Martial," or "A Confederate Veteran Tries to Explain the Event," the Confederate officer is the heroic figure of the biographical reminiscences, the memorial of the lost cause, and the wise old patriarch. Therefore, it seems that the story balances its harshly realistic view with the more romantic visions of family history and childhood reminiscence recollected in reminiscence and in very personal poetry. Richard King observes in his chapter on the southern family romance that grandparents are often idolized by children when they are beginning to reject the authority of their parents. In particular, grandfathers were historically important for the authors in the first generation of the Southern Renaissance, as they often were literal monuments of antebellum grandeur, Civil War glory, and Reconstruction endurance. Warren's complicated relationship with his maternal grandfather adds an authorial dimension to that between the boy and his grandfather here. In a very real sense, Warren learned his romance of southern history at the knee of his grandfather Penn, listening to the old man's war stories and reading his yellowing histories. A half century later, the author was still trying to understand the wisdom of his grandfather in reminiscent poems.

The complex of family relationships and natural images that structure "When the Light Gets Green" also connect the story with others in Warren's short fiction cycle. (Trigg County was the center of the "Tobacco wars" of 1906–7 depicted in Warren's first published fiction, "Prime Leaf," and his first published novel, *Night Rider*.) Tobacco still is the major cash crop of this agricultural region, and, though basically a tough weed, it requires a great deal of labor and luck to realize a good profit from raising a patch. Therefore, in Warren's home country the rhythms and changes of the seasons are marked in relation to the cultivation of dark-fired tobacco, much as in the stories concerned with it.

"When the Light Gets Green" counterpoints two incidents at the two extremes of the tobacco season and the cycle of human life: planting and harvesting, spring and fall, youth and age. The nameless protagonist who narrates the story represents youth, the beginning of the cycle, while the grandfather, Mr. Barden, symbolizes age. Although no exact ages are indicated, the grandfather's stroke takes place in 1914, and he dies four years later in 1918; since he won a silver cup racing one of his horses in 1859, he would have to be at least in his mid-70s. The narrator's age is never given but he seems to be a young boy about the age of Seth in "Blackberry Winter." Of course, nine would prove autobiographically correct as well, for Warren was born in 1905, and, like the author, this narrator spends the summers with his grandfather on his farm.

The now grown protagonist narrates the story from an adult viewpoint, which would put the "present" somewhere about the time of its composition during the Great Depression. This dual viewpoint of child/adult narrator recalls "Blackberry Winter," but it is even more complex in some ways. For example, the opening paragraph makes an immediate distinction between the idealized and a more realistic view of the grandfather.

> My grandfather had a long white beard and sat under the cedar tree. The beard, as a matter of fact, was not very long and not white, only gray, but when I was a child and was away from him at school during the winter, I would think of him, not seeing him in my mind's eye, and say: He has a long white beard. Therefore, it was a shock to me, on the first morning back home, to watch him lean over the dresser toward the wavy green mirror which in his always shadowy room reflected things like deep water riffled by a little wind, and clip his gray beard to a point. It is gray and pointed, I would say then, remembering what I had thought before. (*Circus*, 88).

In the second paragraph, however, the adult narrator connects his grandfather with the greatest Confederate father figure: "with his good nose and pointed gray beard, he looked like Robert E. Lee, without any white horse to ride" (*Circus*, 88). And without his officer's uniform, for now he wears denim pants that hang loosely around his shrunken "hips and backsides" (*Circus*, 88), a sign of age that makes even the young protagonist feel uneasy. Like the dresser mirror, green and wavy with age, his grandfather reflects in the protagonist what he knows he will come to eventually himself, a symbolic relationship much like that of Seth and Old Jebb in "Blackberry Winter."

In his old age, Grandfather Barden has taken in his daughter and son-in-law, the narrator's Aunt Lucy and Uncle Kirby, to help him with the farm. The childless couple seem like surrogate parents in a sense, and it is not clear if the boy has living parents since he considers the farm as "home," and never mentions any other (*Circus*, 88). In any case, Uncle Kirby is a rather feckless sort, not much of a father figure at all. The grandfather, despite his age and shrunken limbs, is associated with a number of masculine symbols. Of course, he wears the patriarchal beard which he trims with a pair of long shears. After this ritual, he "put on a black vest and put his gold watch and chain in the vest and picked up his cob pipe from the dresser top" (*Circus*, 89). His pipe is the subject of a continuing argument with his daughter (who the narrator realizes is really trying to get Uncle Kirby to stop chewing tobacco), but the grandfather continues to assert himself by bringing it to the breakfast table.

After breakfast, the patriarch saddles his mare and rides out to inspect his fields.

> My grandfather rode across the lot and over the rise back of the house. He sat up pretty straight for an old man, holding the bridle in his left hand, and in his right hand a long hickory tobacco stick whittled down to make a walking cane. I walked behind him and watched the big straw hat he wore waggle a little above his narrow neck, or how he held the stick in the middle, firm and straight up like something carried in a parade, or how smooth and slow the muscles in the mare's flanks worked as she put each hoof down in the ground, going up hill. (*Circus*, 90)

The somewhat phallic walking stick seems almost a ceremonial baton or mace of office, especially since a tobacco stick is a long, pointed stake used to gather the large leaves at harvest for hanging and curing. By contrast, Uncle Kirby "always fumed around waving his dibble, his blue shirt already sticking to his arms with sweat" (*Circus*, 90). A "dibble" is a much smaller stick used to punch the small holes for the tobacco plants at setting time. In fact, the narrator refers to the beginning of the tobacco setting. Kirby races about ineffectually until Mr. Barden "on his mare under the trees, still holding the walking cane . . . said 'Why don't you start 'em, sir?'" (*Circus*, 91). This military, magisterial, almost mythic image leads into the long central passage in which the grandfather is romanticized in family myth.

As I indicated above, most details are ones drawn from the life of Warren's grandfather Penn: the horses and silver trophies, the tobacco-buying failure and his "visionary" insistence on paying his debts, his reading of Macaulay and Gibbon, his recitation of Shelley and Tennyson, or his accounts of the battles at Fort Donelson and Fort Pillow. Yet in contrast to all these heroic, romanticized images, the narrator remembers him after all his talk:

> He only talked much in the morning. Almost every afternoon right after dinner, he went to sleep in his chair, with his hands curled up in his lap, one of them holding the pipe that still sent up a little smoke in the shadow, and his head propped back on the tree trunk. His mouth hung open, and under the hairs of his mustache, all yellow with nicotine, you could see his black teeth and his lips that were wet and pink like a baby's. Usually I remember him that way, asleep. (*Circus*, 93)

The story ends with an incident in the late summer of 1914, nearing the time of the tobacco harvest. Like all tobacco farmers, the grandfather fears an unseasonal cold front that could bring damaging hail rather than needed rain. When "the light gets green" (*Circus*, 94), as it does with the approach of a tornadic storm, the old man tramps up and down the front porch "nervous, as a cat" (*Circus*, 93), predicting hail " 'bigger'n minnie balls' " (*Circus*, 94), or Civil War bullets. When hail does come, he turns into the house and a stroke takes him as he pours a drink from "the old silver pitcher" (*Circus*, 94).

Later, after Dr. Blake leaves, the boy visits his grandfather's room and views the old man sleeping as peacefully as when he napped in his chair under the cedars. Yet when he awakes the old man announces his own death sentence. "It's time to die. Nobody loves me." (*Circus*, 95). The boy tries to answer, "Grandpa, I love you," but he hesitates, somehow knowing it is a lie; he finally mouths the words, "not feeling anything" (*Circus*, 95). It is indeed time for the old officer to die, but he lingers on for another four years. In a short coda, again recalling "Blackberry Winter," the narrator tells us they had to sell the farm and move to town. Later Uncle Kirby was killed in France, and Aunt Lucy had to go to work in a store. The last sentence rings much like that in "Blackberry Winter": "I got the letter about my grandfather, who died of flu, but I thought about four years back, and it didn't matter much" (*Circus*, 95).

Clearly, this August storm has the same kind of effect on the young protagonist as the "blackberry winter" of the previous story had on young Seth. A more difficult comparison concerns the adult narrators and of how much each understands of his youthful experience. Perhaps because "When the Light Gets Green" is a less fully developed story, its epiphany of meaning is less fully realized both by the narrator and perhaps by its author. Although the nameless narrator sees something of the failure of the old order and "the slimed foundations" of his culture, he evidences less of the full humanity of his creator. This is evident in his language, in his consistent use of the term "nigger," for example, whereas the adult Seth uses the more polite "Negro." In "When the Light Gets Green," the narrative voice sounds a bit like the more acerbic narrators in stories like "Goodwood Comes Back." Undoubtedly, Warren was aware of the narrative distance he manipulated in both stories, but their juxtaposition in his short-fiction cycle demonstrates not just his talent for storytelling, but his growing maturity as man and writer in the decade between 1935 and 1945.

"Christmas Gift"

Like "When the Light Gets Green," the story that precedes it in the short-fiction cycle, "Christmas Gift" is salvaged from an unpublished novel—in this case, the writer's first, which exists in several versions under the alternate titles *The Apple Tree* and *God's Own Time*. Although the novel is set in a fictional Tennessee town reminiscent of Guthrie, Kentucky, its focus is less autobiographical and less realistic than either "When the Light Gets Green" or the second unpublished novel that was its source. Although "Christmas Gift" is another initiation story, it concerns the small changes that occur in the experience of the 10-year-old son of Milt Alley, the sharecropper whose cow drowns in the flood of "Blackberry Winter." Because the writer behind the story was not as close to this boy's experience, Warren relates this story in an objective third-person style. Although "Christmas Gift" is not as complex in theme and structure as the two stories that precede it, the straightforward, slice-of-life presentation creates subtle epiphanies of meaning that also stand in interesting contrast to the two stories that follow it, "Goodwood Comes Back" and "The Patented Gate and the Mean Hamburger."[14]

"Christmas Gift" is taken almost entirely from chapter 9 of the last version of Warren's first unpublished novel. Of course, the story stands well on its own, undoubtedly the reason that Warren chose it for submission as a separate piece to the *Virginia Quarterly Review*, where it was published in 1937 (and in the *O'Henry Stories* collection for that year as well). However, the background of the novel's plot proves important for overall meaning. Warren's first attempt at long fiction is decidedly a qualified success in terms of both its structure and its effects. Overall, it seems a derivative work in terms of literary manner, if not subject matter. The setting is part of Warren country, but it is depicted more consciously like Hardy's Wessex or Faulkner's Yoknapatawpha. In particular, the book is marked by a sort of straining for shock and drama, for Warren uses incidents of self-mutilation and suicide to add gravity to the tortuous and tortured family saga at his book's center. The characters who seem to be the closest to the author are two college-age friends, one a naive country boy, the other a more worldly wise aesthete; perhaps they represent two sides of the young Warren himself. In the course of the narrative, the innocent protagonist impregnates a young country girl working in town; she returns to her widowed mother who has married a rough sharecropper. When the young woman is about to give birth, just as Christmas approaches, chapter 9 and the short story open. In the novel, Warren attempts traditional Christian symbolism in order to add a note of life and promise to the dark chronicle of the novel's family. This symbolism is suggested by the first word of the title Warren created for this retelling of his earlier chapter, "Christmas Gift," a title not drawn from the novel.

The story's title is important for more than this suggestion of the Nativity, which otherwise cannot be seen directly in the narrative itself. Its second word provides a clue to the story's structure in terms of the several gifts that create the epiphanies of meaning for the 10-year-old protagonist, Sill Alley. It is interesting to note that Warren changed his characters' names for the publication of his short story cycle, creating another connection with "Blackberry Winter" as well as with other stories set in the Black Patch. Sill's name also suggests his relationship with his family and his father, Milt, which proves important because the boy plays a man's role in his half-sister's childbirth. Although not in the story, it seems probable that Milt has refused the errand himself; Sill tells the doctor that his father resents the arrival of his wife's first grandchild. Another clue to the boy's status is his clothing, hand-me-downs from his father, especially "the rusty-felt man's hat he wore" (*Circus*, 96). So in a sense, Sill is taking his father's role, but he is also searching for a sort of surrogate father to aid him with the difficult situations of his half-sister and his mother.

The story opens as he enters town, sitting next to a nameless farmer on a creaking wagon behind a pair of mules "which steamed and were black like wet iron" (*Circus*, 96). They are wet with snowflakes, momentarily white against their black, but the predominant color throughout the story is gray; "a gray light being hung over everything" (*Circus*, 96), indicating the morally ambiguous stance of this slice-of-life. Determined by a harsh naturalism, the characters seem little more than bewildered animals. Consistent patterns of animal imagery reinforce this feeling. For example, the boy has "sharp gray clawlike fingers" and his "tight skin . . . puckered grayly toward the lips" (*Circus*, 97). On the other hand, the characters exhibit some human compassion, as with the fatherly farmer who brings the boy to town and sets him down at the general store to find the doctor.

The scene in the store recalls the Varner store in Faulkner's Frenchman's Bend, not just in terms of physical description, but of a similarly dichotomous naturalistic/humanistic tension. The store's owner, "a big man, whose belly popped the broad leather belt he wore" (*Circus*, 97), greets the boy and draws him into the circle of loafers around the stove. One of them asks Sill "Who are you, pardner?" (*Circus*, 98), but before the boy can answer this friendly question, another man identifies him as "one of Milt Alley's little bastards" (*Circus*, 98). Although the inquirer warns the other to shut up, the smart aleck continues his line of imagery at the boy's announcement of his mission: "them Alleys allus did calf young . . . So they's going to be another little bastard out to Milt's place" (*Circus*, 98). Only the threat of a beating quiets this antagonist, but the exchange prompts the storeowner to warn the boy to hurry on to the doctor's "before they beat hell out of you at home" (*Circus*, 99). Clearly this is a harsh and violent world, where brute power determines the order of things. Yet before the boy leaves the storeowner gives him a handful of striped candy sticks in some recognition of the season and of the boy's difficult situation.

The second half of the story involves the boy and Dr. Small, a middle-aged country practitioner who becomes another surrogate father. Again the doctor seems a character out of Faulkner, a temperate, wise father surrogate, like Ratliff in the Snopes novels. However, when Sill arrives at the doctor's house he is greeted by Mrs. Small who regards him with "a bird-like asperity" (*Circus*, 101). The contrast between the boy and the middle-class comfort of this house in town underlines his difficulty. Particularly noticible are the "plump cupids of painted china" (*Circus*, 101), insipid caricatures of the strong passions that govern the harsh life of the back country.

The doctor, however, proves more open and generous than his suspicious wife. He is willing to undertake the errand, though his wife seems to imply he will never be paid. As they ride out from town, the doctor is concerned about the boy and his family, as well as about the health of the people they pass. He lets the boy brag about his father, an assertion necessary after the insults in the store, even when the boy quotes Milt on Jim Porsum, the farmer they sharecrop for: "My pappy says he's a goddam sheep-snitchin son-a-bitch" (*Circus*, 104). When the doctor rolls a cigarette, the boy watches him until the tobacco sack is passed, the second gift given.

As they smoke, the doctor's horse and buggy take them off the main road through the bottoms and up along a creek into the rough country of the knobs. It is cold and misty in the darkening afternoon. This is poor country, not even fit to grow sassafras, as the boy notes by again quoting his father. Clearly, it represents the gray world of subsistence agriculture and the sharecropping system, as well as a naturalistic universe. Yet the last paragraph of the story sounds another human note. The boy sneaks one of his candy sticks, and though the doctor purposely avoids observing, Sill finally holds out a stick to him. In a sense, though he has met considerable rejection like his father before him, Sill Alley has found enough help to complete his mission and to accept some of the responsibilities of being a man in difficult world. In return, he can share his small share of the world's rewards with the doctor, exchanging the candy for the tobacco. This lesson finally is the real Christmas gift he receives, and Warren's story carefully and effectively presents this subtle epiphany of initiation in the Black Patch.

"Goodwood Comes Back"

After the introductory novella and the opening cluster of three initiation stories, the next pair of stories in Robert Penn Warren's short-fiction cycle offers contrasting views of two American Adams whose protracted initiations into the harsh realities of modern American life end in violence and death. In both "Goodwood Comes Back" and "The Patented Gate and the Mean Hamburger" the central characters are clearly representative types, a baseball star and a yeoman farmer, respectively, who symbolize traditional variations of the rural American dream; even their names, Luke Goodwood and Jeff York, prove symbolic of their ironic treatment. At the same time each protagonist is contrasted with an observing narrator, a foil who views the destroyed adamic character as symbolic of the dangers inherent in uncriticized American myths, particularly as they become manifest in the romance of southern history.

Although the stories thus prove quite similar, they also present many interesting contrasts. Beyond the obvious differences of subject matter and details of plot, the most important contrast is the degree of distance between protagonists and narrators. In turn, this ironic distance seems to depend on the characters' relationship to Warren's own experience, much as in the contrast between the first-person initiation stories "Blackerry Winter" and "When the Light Gets Green." The baseball star of "Goodwood Comes Back" is clearly based on Kent Greenfield, Warren's childhood friend who pitched in the major leagues during the 1920s. Jeff York seems a character constructed both from personal observation of many such men in Warren's own life and from his agrarian vision of the effects of modern American life on the rural South and its central myths. So both stories prove successful, but in different ways: "Goodwood Comes Back" presents more of the complexity of historical reality and reminiscence, while "The Patented Gate and the Mean Hamburger" creates more of the poetic and symbolic force found in the southern family romance.

"Goodwood Comes Back" is constructed from autobiographical materials that must have been important to Warren both personally and professionally, for he treated them in fiction, poetry, and reminiscence. Kent Greenfield, one of the few boyhood friends Warren stayed in touch with over the course of his life, appears as the tragic Jim Hawks in Warren's untitled and unpublished novel written in 1933–34. Next Greenfield's career provided the suggestion for Goodwood's in this story, first published by the *Southern Review* in 1941. Later Kent Greenfield returned as "K." in the reminiscent poem "American Portrait: Old Style," first published in the *New Yorker* in 1976; and he also appears as himself in several of Warren's interviews and reminiscence pieces, notably *A Portrait of a Father* in 1988. Warren's preoccupation with variations on the character of his friend presented in several genres over a period of decades probably demonstrates his symbolic import as a genuine American hero to the maturing writer, as well as his personal importance as a childhood friend and mentor.[15] After all, Kent Greenfield was Guthrie's other hometown "star," one recognized more quickly but just as quickly forgotten. In some sense, the athlete becomes analogous to the writer, quickly used and discarded by the larger American culture.

The facts of Kent Greenfield's life are generally quite close to those of Luke Goodwood. Both were small-town boys, more fond of the woods than of the classroom, and both graduated from sandlot baseball rather than from high school. Like Goodwood, Greenfield spent only a year in the minor leagues before pitching for several seasons for major league teams; like Goodwood, he began well but fell off rapidly when he took to drink. Again, both the real and the fictional ballplayers came back to their hometowns and drifted into relative oblivion. There the parallels end, however, for Kent Greenfield married, settled down, and lived a relatively stable life in Guthrie until his death.

Luke Goodwood becomes an aimless drifter, until a last attempt to achieve his persistent dream of a small "place" in the country leads him into an unhappy marriage and a deadly feud with his brother-in-law. Warren and his narrator draw the obvious ironies from this situation of an American dream turned nightmare, just as they will in the succeeding story, "The Patented Gate and the Mean Hamburger." In fact, the major structuring device in both stories is the tension between the protagonist's biography, the cautionary tale of success and failure, and the narrator's manner of telling that life story in the particular symbolic ordering that seems most important to him. Therefore, both stories become initiations of their narrators when they experience epiphanies of meaning through the lives and deaths of their biographical subjects.

Although "Goodwood Comes Back" is the story of a baseball player, it is not really a baseball story, at least not in the sense of the classic literary treatments of the sport such as Ring Lardner's stories or P. J. Kinsella's novels. Baseball appears only obliquely in the work, for the narrator is not really a baseball player or fan and is rarely present when Goodwood actually plays the game. Rather, baseball is seen as a symbolic sport in the sort of terms used by contemporary baseball critics such as Roger Angell or George Will. Baseball with its bucolic and innocent tradition is presented as a ritual that re-creates our rural roots and celebrates our lost innocence; in particular, it forms a bridge with childhood, as grown men make a profession of a schoolboy's pastime. In this sense, Luke Goodwood's name seems symbolically appropriate, like Bernard Malamud's Roy Hobbs, the hero of his baseball "romance," *The Natural* (1952). Warren's re-creation of Kent Greenfield as Luke Goodwood retains the small-town, "down-home" sound of his friend's name, but adds nature symbolism suggesting the good life in the big woods. Another irony is present, however, as getting "good wood" on the ball means the production of hits by the batter—exactly what a pitcher like Luke tries to avoid. More importantly, the change in Christian names suggests a religious reading, with Luke as a sort of natural saint corrupted and destroyed by the temptations of success American-style.

The story's structure underlines such a reading. The narrator opens with the boyhood games in which he played for the neighborhood team captained by his older friend, Luke, the best pitcher in town. It is particularly interesting to note that in the manuscript Warren edited for the published version of the story, he excised many of the homey, personal details that would later appear in both his reminiscent poem and prose reminiscences of Kent Greenfield. The balance that results creates a much darker picture than the later poetic or prosaic reminiscences, or, evidently, the life on which all of them were based. An example is the opening sequence, where the nameless narrator introduces his hero and himself through the story's central metaphor: "Luke Goodwood always could play baseball, but I never could to speak of" (*Circus*, 108). He then tells of their school playground games, when the narrator only gets to play because he has the "best mitt" and the protection of Luke, the pitcher and captain.

The differences between Luke and the narrator are more fully demonstrated in their contrasting homes. Most obvious in this domestic detail is the contrast between a wild, masculine life and a more feminized order. Hunting camp, farm, and bachelor "pad," the Goodwood house becomes an important index to the problem of defining a masculine role in modern American life. In a sense, Luke is a throwback to an earlier, more heroic era: "Luke was as good a shot as you would ever hope to see . . . when he was hunting he was like they say the Indians were . . . Luke reminded you of an Indian" (*Circus*, 110). So when Luke drifts out of school he leads a lazy, Huck Finn life: hunting, fishing, and playing ball "for little teams around that section" (*Circus*, 111). In contrast, his emasculated father (wounded much like Simon Loveheart in "The Circus in the Attic") and his shiftless brothers prefigure what will happen to Luke in the real world of America during the Roaring Twenties.

The narrator proves more Tom Sawyer than Huck Finn, enjoying his feminized home and school and progressing into his professional life through his studies. In an interesting contrast Luke excels only at penmanship. Perhaps the most intriguing suggestion of this detail is the connection between Luke's other natural skills and the arts of drawing and writing. In other words, Luke Goodwood is a natural artist, as well as a natural ballplayer, and in this he contrasts with his narrator friend who labors to capture his hero in his prose narrative. When Goodwood quickly moves from sandlot to minor league baseball, "The papers called him the Boy Wizard from Alabama" (*Circus*, 111). The hero takes all of his natural energies and channels them into a boys' game that is also a big business; he soon makes $9000 a season playing for the Philadelphia Athletics. This corruption of the purity of sport by money has been a constant theme in American literature, for example, in the several novels and films that focus on the infamous "Black Sox" scandals following the fixing of the 1919 World Series.

Goodwood's Algeresque success story brings him little real reward. He wastes his money on his family, buying fancy radio sets and player pianos. Although he enjoys the baseball games, time hangs heavy on him in the city. He does manage to lease a place outside of the minor-league city "the first year when the Athletics farmed him out to a smaller team" (*Circus*, 116). He then had his bird dogs crated up and expressed to him, after having the leased farm stocked with ring-neck pheasants. In this world between the small town in Alabama and the northern city of Philadelphia Luke can re-create some of the natural life he finds good for him. For that matter, he enjoys spring training in Florida, when he can spend his free time deep-sea fishing and alligator hunting. But in the modern city he has nothing to do except drink. Even after he pitched in the World Series, earning a bonus of $3000, he soon "hit the skids" (*Circus*, 112). In fact, he isn't able to finish the next season. However, he pulls himself together on a trip home, and the next year he is back in the major leagues. Although the newspaper headlines proclaim "*Goodwood Comes Back*" (*Circus*, 112; emphasis Warren's), his recovery doesn't last: "The drink got him, and he was out of the big time game for good and all . . . then he came back home" (*Circus*, 112).

The narrator's retelling of Luke's story follows the pattern of his own life. After the introduction to their boyhood background, the narrator moves quickly through a summary of Goodwood's baseball career. Because they had drifted apart when both left their hometown, his sources of information are newsy letters and newspaper clippings sent by his sister who has married and settled down in their hometown. He then fills in the outlines of the story from occasional trips home and even rarer meetings with Luke.

Their first meeting takes place early in the depression decade, the hangover of the 1930s that followed the national party of the 1920s. However, Goodwood is still trying to continue the party. On an errand downtown, the narrator encounters Luke and a younger companion nearly drunk at midday and on their way to "nigger town . . . where they could get more whiskey . . . and maybe something else" (*Circus*, 113). When Luke invites the narrator along, he declines, thinking to himself he has more "self respect" (*Circus*, 113). In response to a disparaging remark by another downtown loafer, Goodwood scoops up a rock from the roads and whips it like a bullet against a distant telephone pole. The irony of his boast is obvious: "He turned around, grinning pretty sour, and yelled, 'Still got control, boys!'" (*Circus*, 114).

A year later, the narrator again encounters his boyhood hero on another visit home. This time Goodwood is at least sober, having been shocked by his mother's death from cancer, though shiftless as ever, and he loafs on the sister's lawn "lying relaxed all over just like an animal" (*Circus*, 115). After reminiscing about their boyhood games and hunts, Luke goes on to recount his big-league victories and midadventures. His thesis is that "all pitchers are crazy as hell one way or the other" (*Circus*, 117). For example, he roomed with another pitcher on the road who would play with electric trains and mechanical autos; this other pitcher liked toy boats best of all, and kept Goodwood awake half the night splashing in the bathtub. Another pitcher, a "Polak" from the Pennsylvania coal fields, liked to pick up women and start fights in roadhouses. After being thrown out of one roadhouse, he assembled a pile of baseball-sized rocks and knocked out all the windows, injuring a woman with a rock in the process. Of course, Goodwood provides his own best example of childish behavior, ruining his chance at success with alcohol, and being reduced to his aimless life in his hometown.

Luke Goodwood is not without plans, however. He is trying to get the money together to buy a country place where he can "farm a little and hunt and fish" (*Circus*, 118). When he explains his plan to the narrator, they conjure up the vision of a town character, old Mr. Bullard, who lives by himself in a cabin by the river. Yet Luke never has to become this sort of caricature of himself. Six months later he marries a country girl, probably because of her half-interest in a farm, out in "the real hoot-owl sticks" (*Circus*, 119). Of course, Goodwood is not cut out for marriage, and the narrator supposes "she got to riding him about the way he spent his time, off hunting and all" (*Circus*, 119). In any case, "bad blood" developed with his brother-in-law, who had the other half-interest in the farm and who kills Luke with his own shotgun. The final sentences punctuate this grim conclusion: "He shot him three times, the gun was a .12 guage pump gun, and you know what even one charge of a .12 gauge will do at a close range like a kitchen" (*Circus*, 119). Goodwood will not come back this time.

Of course, it is precisely at this point that Warren's story departs from its autobiographical sources. Kent Greenfield, the model for Luke Goodwood, married and settled down to a long if unspectacular life, so a more gentle sort of loss and irony pervades the reminiscent poetry and prose in which Warren later recalled Greenfield. During the depression years, Warren naturally gravitated to more negative and violent images of the failure of dreams, both personal and cultural. Greenfield's first incarnation, Jim Hawks of the unpublished autobiographical novel, also dies at the hands of his murderous partner. So too do the symbolic heroes of his first published novels that had their beginnings in the same period: Perse Munn of *Night Rider*, Bogan Murdock of *At Heaven's Gate*, and Willie Stark of *All the King's Men*. Images of violence and death becoming indices of cultural disorder are also found in the shorter fiction, as we have seen in "The Circus in the Attic" and the initiation stories, and as we will discover in the story poised after "Goodwood Comes Back," "The Patented Gate and the Mean Hamburger."

"The Patented Gate and the Mean Hamburger"

The stories of composite experiences made into exemplary lives some distance from Warren's own experience are even more closely focused on the symbolic rendering of cultural failures. The fictional Luke Goodwood, like the real Kent Greenfield, existed within a tradition of adamic Americans. Jeff York, the protagonist of "The Patented Gate and the Mean Hamburger," is an even more perfect example of the dangers inherent in uncritical acceptance of American dreams and southern romance. Goodwood suggested the inadequacy of the dreams of an edenic wilderness created by Cooper, Thoreau, and Twain, while York dramatizes the failure of the visions of agrarian utopias posited by Jefferson, Emerson, and Whitman. Both protagonists actually re-create more closely the fallen American Adams of Hemingway, Fitzgerald, or Faulkner.[16]

One key to Jeff York's symbolic status is his suggestive name, which proves important in two ways. First of all, it is one point of differentiation between him and the character type he represents; in fact, the tension between individual and type becomes a major structuring device in the story. Second, the protagonist's name resonates with important historical allusions that locate his type within American contexts. His name is typical of its region, the fictional Cobb County, Tennessee, evidently somewhere on the Cumberland Plateau, if not the Black Patch. Aside from its more general white, Anglo-Saxon, Protestant resonance, the name York is an important one in Tennessee. Sergeant Alvin York of Fentress County in the Upper Cumberland country had become America's greatest hero during World War I; a sort of folk hero, he was a pacifist who, when forced to fight by circumstances, decimated and captured a German machine-gun company. After the war, York returned to Tennessee where he was caught up in the turbulent politics of the 1920s. A similar character, Private Porsun, appears in Warren's second published novel, *At Heaven's Gate*. Jeff York might well have been kin to the famous sergeant of the same name, as he exhibits similar mountaineer skills and traditional values, in particular a stubborn self-reliance.

The protagonist's Christian name proves even more intriguing in historical association. It is most likely short for Jefferson, a first name common in the region as a distant reflection of our first democratic president. In any case, it certainly suggests Thomas Jefferson, and in ideological terms, Jeff York lives out the Jeffersonian ideal. He is a yeoman farmer who has raised himself by dint of hard work and self-sacrifice from sharecropper to property owner. Of course, Jefferson was an important symbolic figure in several of Warren's works, most notably in *Brother to Dragons*, which ponders the brutal murder of a slave by the president's own nephews, a crime never mentioned by Jefferson in his writings. Warren's intellectual admiration for Jefferson is tempered by his recognition of the difficulty of the great democrat's belief in the perfectability of human nature. Like *Brother to Dragons*, "The Patented Gate and the Mean Hamburger" unites a number of texts and symbols to demonstrate the failure of the Jeffersonian version of the American Dream.

Of course, this particular manifestation of Jeffersonian man lost in modern America takes place in Tennessee and involves the romance of southern history. Warren works particularly hard to connect his protagonist with the universals of the southern yeoman. Jeff York's description, for example, emphasizes his representation of a type, the yeoman close to nature, land, family, and tradition. The narrator notes, "You have seen him a thousand times" (*Circus*, 120). Warren's opening sentence connects the individual and the type, as well as narrator and reader, in the context of the little county-seat town on Saturday afternoon. In his essay on writing the story (reprinted in Part 2) Warren reveals that it is based on the life and death of a real farmer from his native region, a man the writer had seen many times.

The description of Jeff York that follows is at once photographic and poetic in its balance of details. He wears a coat with overalls, a realistic combination; the coat is wool, while the denim is "washed to pale pastel blue like the color of the sky after a shower in spring" (*Circus*, 120). His very body reflects the textures of nature as well: "His long wrist bones hang out from the sleeves of the coat, the tendons showing along the bone like the dry twist of grapevine still corded on the stove-length of a hickory sapling you would find in his wood box beside his cookstove among the split chunks of gum and red oak" (*Circus*, 120). His face (and presumably his neck) are "a dull red like the red clay mud or clay dust which clings to the bottom of his pants . . . or a red like the color of a piece of hewed cedar which has been left in the weather" (*Circus*, 120). In fact, his face seems as impassive as if it was "molded from the clay or hewed from the cedar" (*Circus*, 120). His eyes "are squinched up like eyes accustomed to wind or sun or to measuring the stroke of the ax or to fixing the object over the rifle sights" (*Circus*, 121). Standing by the court square, York's eyes disdain "the world which passes under their level gaze as a rabble passes under the guns of a rocky citadel around whose base a slatternly town has assembled" (*Circus*, 121).

This heroic simile introduces the town that flows around him, contrasting with Jeff in his stoic stillness, as well as his slatternly wife and his three "towheaded children." As in "Christmas Gift," the real heart of the town is the general store, and here Jeff and his family do their trading. Whereas everything associated with Jeff York is redolent of nature, the town is connected with unnatural imagery: it is a place of cement and cast iron, of "beer parlors" (*Circus*, 121), and "dog-wagons" (*Circus*, 125).

The Saturday ritual of hamburgers at the dogwagon, or short-order diner, develops another major contrast of the story first introduced in the title. The long introduction to the southern yeoman as a type emphasizes the same closeness to nature as emerges from the specific description of Jeff York. For the protagonist is not only like a thousand others in his region, he is the scion of a long line of archetypal forebears: Jeff stands or hunkers down with others of his sort by the square because "his father had stood with their fathers and his grandfather with their grandfathers" (*Circus*, 122). The narrator, more like a social historian, traces their movement all the way from the Atlantic coast across the mountains and into the hard-scrabble country of the interior. If they stayed in Cobb County and didn't push further west, say to the Ozarks, they stayed on the unproductive ridges as "half woodsman" or came down into the richer bottom lands as sharecroppers. In fact, in his own essay on the story Warren reveals that he had recently read a social history of the South that made these very points. Warren himself connected them with the rural-to-urban migration that had just taken place during World War II.

Jeff York is different, for "he had broken the curse" (*Circus*, 123). After three decades of hard work from age 20 to age 50, "Jeff York had a place" (*Circus*, 122). Of course, his place was not very good, but his years of sweat and self-denial have made it into a fine little farm almost free of debt. Over these years he has restored the gullied fields, mended the broken fences, and rebuilt the barn and house. "Last, he put up a gate" (*Circus*, 124). The gate provides the first half of Warren's title and serves as a symbol for Jeff himself. As the narrator sums it up, "The gate was the seal Jeff York had put on all the years of sweat and rejection" (*Circus*, 124). As such, it proves a complex symbol. Obviously, it confers a sense of ownership and success. One of Jeff's neighbors observed him at night riding his mule back and forth through the gate, testing its mechanism and enjoying his possession. Although the gate seems a natural symbol of a farmstead, it is also mechanical, a product of the urban present. Warren sums up the gate in his essay on the story: "The gate is 'patented'-clever, efficient, belonging, if you will, to the world of the modern, to the town, or rather, to the prosperous farms beginning to be oriented toward town."[17]

The dramatized scenes in the present develop the other half of the symbolic title, "the mean hamburger." As the gate is associated with Jeff, summing up the long narration about him as an archetype that opens the story, the second, dramatic half of the story involves his wife and the town's hamburger stand. Jeff's wife, who is given no name other than Mrs. York, is a country woman some 20 years younger than Jeff. She too is associated with nature in the description that introduces her. She is a small woman with dark eyes "which were surprisingly bright in that sidewise, secret flicker, like the eyes of a small, cunning bird which surprise you from the brush" (*Circus*, 124). These nature images replay those used for her husband, but with a negative quality. For example, in the winter she wears a wool coat "with a scrap of fur at the collar which looked like some tattered growth of fungus feeding on old wood" (*Circus*, 124). When she wears high-heeled shoes in town, she seems like a trained animal learning a new trick. In fact, it soon becomes apparent that Mrs. York is much more interested in town than in country.

After all, her life with Jeff York is a hard one almost by necessity, with only a few spots of life, of color here or there. Chief among these is the Saturday hamburger after their shopping in town. As the narrator puts it, "when they get to town and get hold of beef and wheat bread and all the stuff to jack up the flavor, they have to swallow to keep the mouth from flooding even before they take the first bite" (*Circus*, 126). His description is suggestive of contemporary "fast food," but in the middle 1930s such fare is dispensed only in "dogwagons," like "Slick Hardin's *Dew Drop Inn Diner*. The diner was built like a railway coach, but it was set on a concrete foundation . . . at each end the concrete was painted to show wheels" (*Circus*, 126; emphasis Warren's)." Again the images of modern, mechanical, mobile life prove more interesting, and they reflect the personality of the owner and propriator, Slick Hardin. This figure (reminiscent of Faulkner's Popeye) is a local hero, a person "with the air of romance about him" (*Circus*, 126). Slick had for a few years been a preliminary fighter over in Nashville, before he returned to his hometown. Now, however, he is tired of "slinging hash to them hicks" (*Circus*, 130), and he wants to sell the diner and buy a beer parlor back in Nashville. In many ways, Hardin, the contemporary slickster manipulating a caricature of masculinity to promote himself and his rootless life-style, is the antithesis of York.

Not surprisingly, given this triangle of characters, Mrs. York is taken with Hardin and his enterprise. In the first dramatized scene, Slick banters with her as he serves up her order: "Yeah, if I liked them hamburgers much as you, I'd buy me a hamburger stand" (*Circus*, 128). Although Jeff at first reacts angrily to him, his anger turns against his wife when she asks Slick's price. On the following Thursday, she sneaks back into town and repeats the scene without the company of her husband. Although Slick thought he was putting her on in the opening scene, this time she prevails as he tries to justify his asking price of $1450. A week later the third dramatized scene has Jeff York in the local bank, selling his farm in order to buy the hamburger stand.

The narrator, functioning as a sort of chorus for the town, speculates on how she persuaded him to replace his vision with hers. Did she nag him or refuse her wifely duties?: "She was a small, dark, cunning woman with a sidewise look from her lowered face, and she could have thought up ways of her own, no doubt" (*Circus*, 131). Slick Hardin in a sense puts his seal of approval on her; after she cooks an order under his tutelage, he tells her, "lady you sure fling a mean hamburger" (*Circus*, 132).

Slick, true to type, leaves on the evening train. Jeff works to make the diner like his farm; he cleans up the trash, paints the place white, and changes its sign. Then one Sunday he walks out to view his farm and hangs himself from his patented gate. In the single-paragraph coda that follows, Mrs. York proves true to her destiny as well. She makes a success of the diner, learns to walk in high heels, and fixes herself up. The railroad men and the pool-hall loafers favor the place: "they said, she flung a mean hamburger" (*Circus*, 133). In his essay on the story, Warren tells us he meant the adjective both in the slang sense that Slick intended, but also in the more traditional sense of "cruel, ferocious, destructive" ("Gate," 266). Certainly, the symbols of modern urban life are all that and more for the Jeff Yorks of the changing South.

"A Christian Education"

"A Christian Education," the seventh selection in Robert Penn Warren's short-fiction cycle, proves important in several ways, which might explain its central position. It is interesting to note that Warren deliberately placed the story at midpoint of the volume, swapping it with "Her Own People" in the galley proofs. "A Christian Education" works a good deal better as a pivotal tale, for it offers many connections with other stories. Most important, it is another initiation story narrated by an adult who is just becoming conscious of his own "Christian education," so it suggests themes and structures encountered in "Blackberry Winter" and "When the Light Gets Green." However, the emphasis here is more on other characters who become symbolic to the narrator, as in "Goodwood Comes Back" or "The Patented Gate and the Mean Hamburger." The story's Christian symbolism also recalls "Christmas Gift," particularly in the ambiguity of both titles, and points forward to the religious imagery of "The Confession of Brother Grimes." Of course, "The Circus in the Attic" provided the general background for this story of ambivalent revelations and epiphanies in the Black Patch.[18]

The story was first published by *Mademoiselle*, a slick magazine for younger women, in 1945, the era in which Warren wrote "Blackberry Winter." However, manuscript evidence indicates the story is probably a decade older, dating from the period of "When the Light Gets Green" and "Goodwood Comes Back." Like those stories, the narrative is less conscious of itself than "Blackberry Winter," with less sense of its own meaning realized by the narrator; however, like Warren's most famous tale, this one turns on carefully manipulated archetypal symbolism. Warren dramatizes only one actual scene in this short short story, the accidental drowning of Silas Nabb at the Methodist Sunday school picnic. The first half of the story provides social background and religious context, then the single dramatized scene moves inexorably to Silas's death and the narrator's abortive attempt to recover Silas's body from the depths of the pond. Although he "likely dived near fifty times" (*Circus*, 141), he fails to recover the body and gives up the search.

Even though this failed attempt at recovery provides only a small part of the whole picnic/drowning scene, indeed of the lives of the Nabb family and the narrator, it is the symbolic heart of the story. When the narrator reaches the bottom on his second dive, the scene suddenly becomes almost surrealistic. The images of depth and darkness, smoothness and softness create an instantaneous recognition of our ambiguous relation to death: "I thought how nice it would be to lie there, it was so soft, and look up trying to see where the light made the water green" (*Circus*, 141). On a later dive, he touches the face of Silas's corpse, and confesses that he "felt like screaming, but you can't scream underwater but once" (*Circus*, 142). In other words, the deep dives into the pond take on the aspect of a Melvillean initiation, a night journey into the depths, in which the narrator comes to recognize his own mortality. Since this experience becomes his real education, it works ironically against the title. Rather than a Christian education, so prized by the proud Mr. Nabb, the narrator receives a naturalistic epiphany of meaning as he touches death in the depths of the pond.

This reading of the central incident is reinforced by the story's long introduction and brief conclusion. The story opens not with the narrator, but with the Nabb family. Mr. Nabb, "a successful farmer," is also the superintendant of the Sunday school at the Methodist church. The narrator notes that he "can recollect the time when I was a boy and used to go to church" (*Circus*, 134). Part of his recollection is of Mr. Nabb, a "little man . . . his face being smooth and pink like a boy's . . . his voice . . . mighty high like a woman's" (*Circus*, 134). This description connects him closely to the rest of his family. Mrs. Nabb is one of "those big fat women who ail all the time and cry if you look at them" (*Circus*, 135). Silas, their only child for 11 years, "just wasn't right bright" (*Circus*, 136); in fact, he becomes Mr. Nabb's cross to bear.

Therefore, the Nabbs resolve to have another child, though Mrs. Nabb has difficulty getting "in the family way" (*Circus*, 135). "Anyway, it took Mr. Nabb eleven more years before he got any results" (*Circus*, 135). It is interesting to note that Warren's manuscript naturalistically mentions "eleven more years of humping." Probably censorship caused the deletion, as the vernacular expression complements the "miracle" of Mrs. Nabb's new conception. Since the narrator started in the same Sunday-school class as Silas, he must like him be about "thirteen or fourteen years old" (*Circus*, 138) during the summer of the fateful picnic, an age to be interested in sex, in the drives of life as well as of death.

Although Silas falls behind in public school, he is promoted in the Sunday school in which his father supervises and his mother teaches. "He could say the Golden Text sometimes, though, if he got a little prompting from his mother" (*Circus*, 136). However, he seems to have learned only one lesson: turning the other cheek. All of the other boys take advantage of the slow, hulking Silas. If pressed for a reason, Silas answers, "God says not to fight" (*Circus*, 137). The narrator even joins in the taunts: "Did God say that? You know I didn't hear him say nothing" (*Circus*, 137). At the fateful picnic, the boys are forced to take Silas along with them in the Nabbs' rowboat. Perhaps feeling cramped, Silas finally reacts to their taunts and pulls a pocketknife, "which his father didn't have any better sense than to give him one Christmas" (*Circus*, 139). This "Christmas gift" negates Silas's abortive Christian education, for in the struggle that follows he falls overboard and drowns.

The narrator describes these events in terms of his own vision of himself: "I always figured I would like to save somebody's life sometime and be a hero" (*Circus*, 140). Of course, he fails, but when an older fellow finds the body on his third try, the narrator is secretly relieved: "for if I was the one to get it up, Mr. Nabb might have thought I was good enough to save Silas when he fell in" (*Circus*, 142).

Even the Nabbs rather quickly accept Silas's death as "God's will" (*Circus*, 141).

And, of course, they have their three year old, Alec, for comfort. In a single-paragraph coda, the narrator reveals that Alec, though plenty bright, turned out to be a sorrow of another sort for the poor Nabbs. He would have none of the "other cheek" business; rather, "He wouldn't take anything off nobody" (*Circus*, 142). When he was 22, he killed another man in a fight and was sentenced to a long term "in Nashville in the pen" (*Circus*, 142).

Alec Nabb's fate recalls that of Little Jebb in "Blackberry Winter," who also killed a man in a struggle and wound up in prison. However, a comparison of the two codas demonstrates significant differences in depth, tone, and the degree of insight of the narrators. Like the narrators of "When the Light Gets Green" or "Goodwood Comes Back," the boy who dove for Silas Nabb's body in the depths of the pond has learned some important things about death and life. Still, he seems less aware that both Silas and Alec are in a sense his surrogate brothers, one killed and the other a killer. In turn, Mr. and Mrs. Nabb are surrogate parents, but they provide no more insights into the true nature of life and death than his own parents. In other words, the narrator's education, both religious and secular, proves deficient. Although he senses the meaning of the Nabbs in his own life, he can only articulate the more obvious ironies of the situation, much in the manner of the narrator of the story that precedes "A Christian Education," "The Patented Gate and the Mean Hamburger." The next two stories that follow in the second half of the book present two more initiations, more or less ambivalent than this narrator's "Christian Education."

"The Love of Elsie Barton: A Chronicle"

The next two stories, "The Love of Elsie Barton: A Chronicle" and "Testament of Flood" are paired for several reasons. First of all, they involve the same characters, narratives, and settings, and, though each can stand well on its own, they are clearly interrelated. This relation, in turn, derives from their common source in Robert Penn Warren's untitled, unpublished, somewhat autobiographical novel discussed above as the source of "When the Light Gets Green." The novel was the second Warren had written, probably in 1933–34 while teaching at Vanderbilt. It is not clear if the author ever sent the novel out for publication, though it seems publishable in terms of the standards of the period. He quickly used parts of the narrative for stories: "Testament of Flood" appeared in the *Magazine* in 1935. "The Love of Elsie Barton: A Chronicle" was published later, in 1946, in *Mademoiselle*, though it appears the story was written and unsuccessfully circulated in the mid-1930s. The tightly organized "Testament of Flood" proves much the better story in its own right; "The Love of Elsie Barton: A Chronicle," as its title indicates, remains more a long narrative, more like a part of a novel or an abortive novel, than a fully realized short story or novella.[19]

"Testament of Flood" proves stronger and more tightly focused because it, like the novel from which it was condensed, is centered on the epiphany of meaning its autobiographical protagonist draws from his relationship with his attractive classmate, Helen Beaumont. The symbolically named Steve Adams seems like a youthful version of his creator, just as his family re-creates the Warrens, and his hometown resembles Guthrie, Kentucky. Steve develops from boy to man in terms of his frustrated love for Helen and his lost friendship with Jim Hawks, another incarnation of Kent Greenfield. These two characters are connected through the sinister Frank Barber, a dissolute, perhaps disturbed, veteran of the "Great War" who uses his position as a railroad detective to cover up a series of petty crimes. Frank seduces and then brutalizes Helen, and he kills Jim in a falling-out over the plundering of a railroad boxcar. Steve's development is also assisted by his father, a man much like Thomas Warren, and grandfather, a patriarch modeled on Warren's grandfather Penn, recalling "When the Light Gets Green." Another surrogate father is Mr. Griffin, Steve's high school teacher, who proves an important, if flawed, mentor.

The secondary line of the novel's plot concerns Steve's love interest, Helen Beaumont. She is a strange, wistful, seductive girl, in many ways the opposite of Steve Adams; she seems somehow fallen from grace even as a high school student. In other words, she becomes a character from romantic narrative motivated by her identity as the product of the illicit passion between her mother, Elsie Barton, and the rakish Benjamin Beaumont. In an interesting twist of plot, Thomas Adams, Steve's father, had loved Elsie as a girl, losing her to the more worldly and forceful Beaumont just as Steve loses Helen to the older, harder Barber. The feckless Beaumont took little interest in his family and died when his daughter was only 10, so Helen is raised by her mother, who becomes a recluse within the closed world of the small town. The overall situation resembles Hawthorne's romance *The Scarlet Letter*, for Helen, like little Pearl, develops in the shadow of her mother's past love; unlike Pearl, though, she is not rescued from the past but compelled by it into a destructive relationship.

The two interrelated stories drawn from this unpublished novel are arranged in chronological order, beginning with Elsie Barton and her love, then moving to Helen Beaumont and hers. However, within the stories themselves we discover a complex relationship of time levels, much as in the novel from which these pieces are drawn. Overall, the untitled novel follows the course of a school year, and it makes symbolic use of the natural cycles of the year and of human life by shifting through time by means of flashbacks and flashforwards. So the first of the paired stories chronicles Elsie Barton's life from the flood of springlike passion to the dry season of age; in a sense, Helen is the testament of that earlier flood, and her story is associated with burgeoning spring as well. Therefore, the overall structures of these two stories, both as individual pieces and as interrelated texts, can be understood in the contrast between the linear evolution of time found in a chronicle and the cycles of life that impart meaning to the line of time.

The relationships between history, narrative, and natural cycle prove complex in the chronicle of Elsie Barton and her love. The story opens in the present of the novel, the early 1930s, but ranges back to Elsie's birth some "fifty years before" (*Circus*, 143). Her father, a Confederate officer, moved to Charlestown, Tennessee, after the Civil War, opened a store, and married a local girl. Elsie's childhood was unexceptional, except that her father sent her off to a Baptist boarding school in Kentucky. She returned after her mother died from a cut on a rusty butcher knife, in an image recalling the death of the narrator's father in "Blackberry Winter." While keeping house for her father, Elsie is courted in turn by Thomas Adams, an unremarkable local boy, and Benjamin Beaumont, an older man from Kentucky. Beaumont seduces (indeed, almost rapes), impregnates, and marries Elsie in 1900, and she gives birth to a daughter, Helen, in the summer of 1901. The husband and father dies a decade later, of a stroke in a Nashville hotel room, while evidently off on a spree. When Helen blossoms in her senior year of high school almost another decade later "half the boys and young men had been wild over her (*Circus*, 145), including Steve Adams—as we learn in "Testament of Flood." However, Helen is taken with Frank Barber, "who was nearly fifteen years older" (*Circus*,

145), a romantic, dangerous figure recalling Benjamin Beaumont. Unlike her mother's life and the plot of the novel from which the story is derived, Helen throws over her older lover, leaves Charlestown after high school, and evidently leads a normal life "up north." After her daughter departs, Elsie becomes the recluse we met at the opening of the story, who leaves her home only to go to her job as a bookkeeper for the local feedstore.

The narrative pattern through which this linear history is presented is complicated. Once again the narrator is part of the community, a choruslike figure much as in "The Patented Gate and the Mean Hamburger." His narration moves back into Elsie's past as far as Helen's departure for the North. He then notes that the town slowly forgets the whole story: "So the life of Elsie Beaumont, who had been Elsie Barton, slowly achieved its perfect form, like a crystal growing to its ineluctable pattern, in a solution kept in a still bottle" (*Circus*, 147). The larger part of the story traces Elsie Barton's development back to Helen's birth, then moves further back to her own childhood in the early 1880s and forward again to her marriage in 1901. The purpose of this complex narrative pattern seems to echo the title: the story concerns the life and love of Elsie Barton. In fact, the town calls her "Miss Elsie" (*Circus*, 142), a usage still common in the region for older unmarried women, forgetting that she had ever been Mrs. Beaumont. The image of the crystal becomes important here; the basic pattern is determined at its origin no matter what accretions take place during its existence.

The basic pattern of Elsie's story exists in the cycle of the seasons, including the prevalent images of water, both of which are also found in "Testament of Flood." When Elsie is courted by Thomas Adams, she responds coldly to his declaration of love, yet she thought she might marry him: "She had simply realized that it would probably come to pass, like growing old, like the turn of a season" (*Circus*, 152). Her life seems to follow its natural cycles just as the seasons of the year motivate its particular events. For example, Benjamin Beaumont seduces her in August 1900. His invitation to ride with him on an errand into the country is fraught with romantic significance, and she surprises herself by agreeing to go along: "With the still air enveloping the world, with the houses around shuttered for the afternoon, with the silence and the hypnotic pulsation of the heat, that day was, perhaps, the one day in her life when she would have said yes, and gone with him" (*Circus*, 155). When Beaumont "assaults" her "without premeditation, really without passion" (*Circus*, 156), in her thoughts she heard "her name, 'Elsie Barton' . . . over and over . . . with that dull asseveration of her identity" (*Circus*, 157). Meanwhile, Beaumont feels the loss of what love he had for her "because he had dried up that obscure and thin, but pure spring of sentiment that Elsie Barton had provoked in him" (*Circus*, 157). These symbolic interlacings of personal identity and natural cycles persist throughout the story.

The same combinations of images are present in Warren's description of Helen's development as well. When she suddenly blossoms as the town's beauty, she also acquires her father's bold stare; the townspeople comment: "Just like her pappy . . . she's got her pappy's look" (*Circus*, 145). As the narrator puts it, "for suddenly with the girl grown up among them, like spring come all at once after the last cold spell, they remembered how Benjamin Beaumont had had that straight look" (*Circus*, 145). In the springtime of her life, as well as the spring semester of her senior year in high school, her relationship with Frank Barber grows into a romance: "People said they bet he was making some time and he wasn't riding out in the country to see how the crops were coming" (*Circus*, 145). But unlike her mother who was seduced in summer (and unlike the novel from which the story is derived), Helen drops Frank, though he continues to pursue her; indeed, one of the town's father figures, tough "Old Mr. Dick Bailey" (*Circus*, 146) has to frighten Frank off. "Then, just as the leaves began to turn, she left . . . and never came back" (*Circus*, 146).

This last development is the most significant change from the novel, in which Helen married Frank and bore his child only a few months later. Perhaps Warren made the change in order to contrast mother and daughter, to break the cyclic patterns, and, most importantly, to demonstrate that Elsie Barton was trapped not by history, nature, or romance, but by being Elsie Barton. Her insistence on a fixed identity symbolized in her name recalls Louise Bolton from "The Circus in the Attic." Like the earlier Louise, she puts a "bolt on" her affections, really loving neither parents, suitors, nor child. In fact, this in-turning identity may well be the most important irony of the story's ambiguous title. Elsie Barton's chronicle is concerned finally with self-love.

Her "grand passion," the love of her life with Benjamin Beaumont, is an empty relationship that she indulged more out of vanity than any other reason. The other girls of the town envied her relationship with the tall Kentuckian, whereas they were not concerned with Thomas Adams at all. She enjoys neither Beaumont's kisses nor his more ardent embraces which continue throughout the autumn, and she is unhappy with her pregnancy, her marriage, and her wedding night. The story ends away from Charlestown, at the Beaumont farm in central Kentucky. Here she must perforce relate to Old Man Beaumont, an "old, somewhat shrunken, more violent, more profane Benjamin" (*Circus*, 161). Although he is kind enough to her in his way, she is rather disgusted by him. When she leaves after a year to return to Charlestown, she bursts into tears not because she will miss him, but because he represents what her husband will become: "some blind, brutish force which would trample her and pound her" (*Circus*, 162). When her husband dies she stands expressionless at his funeral, her tears already shed. She never decorates his grave, "and the weeds grew ranker, year by year" (*Circus*, 144).

These images of her withdrawn, autumnal life opened her story: "She was so still and withered . . . a small woman wearing a baggy man's sweater" (*Circus*, 143). Her facial expression is peculiarly still, "with the stillness of water carried in an old pail" (*Circus*, 143). Her house, which no one else has entered in 15 years, presents the same expressionless face to the world with the shades always drawn in winter, the lights out in summer, her porch concealed by a screen of "moonvine." Although rumors persist about her strange habits of living, eating out of cans and such, no one really knows or cares about her. Even the letters from Helen, postmarked from several northern cities, become less frequent and then cease. Finally, Elsie Barton becomes like "the dead lumber and drift of her life that she had accumulated in the garret under her dry roof" (*Circus*, 150), part of the detritus of life in the town.

So ends the chronicle of Elsie Barton. Although the narrative inverts the order of events, and natural cycles add other meanings to them, her history essentially gives the lie to southern romance. Elsie is at once a caricature of both the southern heroine of popular romance and Hester Prynne, the romantic heroine of Hawthorne's *The Scarlet Letter*. Her love is devoid of passion; if anything it is only self-love, denying all the characterization of the romantic heroine. Unlike Hawthorne's Hester she neither redeems nor is redeemed by her love or by its symbol, Helen, and her reclusion serves no personal nor social utility as in Hester's case. Both Elsie Barton and Benjamin Beaumont are as much victims of the romance of southern history as their namesake, Jeremiah Beaumont, the protagonist of Warren's later novel *World Enough and Time*, a parallel emphasized by the similar descriptions in both story and novel of the Beaumont farms. When we remember that Warren connected his *World Enough and Time* with Hawthorne and his materials, it is easy to see that this particular sort of southern romance was a part of Warren's work almost from the beginning of his career.

"Testament of Flood"

"Testament of Flood" is a more tightly structured story than its companion piece. Although it condenses a much greater portion of the unpublished novel that provides the matrix for both stories, it manages the task with a good deal more concision, particularly in terms of symbolic texts within the narrative itself. In a sense, it proves a more fully rewritten story as well. Elsie Barton's chronicle comes almost entire from chapter 4 of the untitled novel, with a small piece from chapter 2 for an opening followed by a summary of the novel's action. "Testament of Flood" also telescopes that action, and though it uses short pieces of several chapters, these are thoroughly rewritten and integrated. At the same time "Testament of Flood" is another initiation story, and it is centered more precisely in the epiphany of meaning for its protagonist, Steve Adams.

This central figure is Warren's adamic and autobiographical protagonist in the unpublished and untitled novel. Steve also becomes the central consciousness of the story, as Warren's revision angles the narration through the character. For example, the story's first sentence echoes that of its companion piece, but the emphasis shifts to the boy's consciousness: "So dry, so withered, she appeared as she went up and down the street that the boy, meeting her, could scarcely believe her the subject of those narratives inconclusively whispered now and then by ladies who came to see his mother" (*Circus*, 163). It is also interesting to contrast this sentence with the novel's text, which makes Elsie the subject "of the comment which the ladies who came to see his mother made in their guarded or captious voices." The word "narratives" suggests that Elsie is not so much the subject of social or historical commentary as she is of storytelling and mythologizing. In other words, as analysis of her chronicle demonstrated, Elsie Barton became part of the romance of southern history.

The last sentence of the story's opening paragraph condenses the patterns of history, narrative, and natural cycles that structured Elsie Barton's chronicle: "So dry, she was like those bits of straw or trash lodged innocently in the branches of creek-bottom sycamores as testament of long-subsided spring flood—a sort of high water mark of passion in the community" (*Circus*, 163). Of course, the analysis of the companion story demonstrated how the image of the spring flood and the source of the story's title is drawn from the romantic consciousness of the town, as passion proves to be a sadly mistaken name for Elsie's love. This juxtaposition of flood and trash recalls Warren's most successful initiation story, "Blackberry Winter," where the flood and its destructive wake also symbolized the wrenching childhood realization of death and destruction. (Flood serves a similar symbolic purpose in both the long poem *Brother to Dragons* and the novel *Flood*, which is subtitled *A Romance of Our Time*.) It is important to note that the protagonist knows the flood only by rumor—he sees only the detritus of the past, the autumnal bits of trash.

In the second paragraph, the protagonist, here still "the boy," discovers "a more convincing memento. . . . It was the girl" (*Circus*, 163). The girl is Helen Beaumont, Elsie Barton's daughter by Benjamin Beaumont, now suddenly blossomed into a full-blown beauty and beloved by the dissolute and dangerous Frank Barber. However, the order of narration does not move to any of these details, but instead to a long, careful description of the girl mailing a letter. As this scene is not found in the novel, Warren must have created it for this position in the story. Therefore we must recognize the passage as an important crux in the narrative. Although it seems more likely that the girl is merely mailing the letter for her mother, some bit of business from the feedstore, the boy speculates that "she herself might have written it" (*Circus*, 164). He imagines it to be an "intimate" message, signed only "Helen," in a hand he would recognize from her schoolwork. Most of all, he is conscious that the letter "never belonged to him" (*Circus*, 164). In other words, this interpolated passage creates a romantic image of a text within that narrative, an image of the romantic text that Steve Adam creates from the history of Helen Beaumont, just as the town created one from the history of Elsie Barton.

This long passage ends with his recollections of Helen carrying the letters to the post office, despite the fact that he can see her every day sitting in the senior classroom at the local high school. The narrative now shifts to the classroom, the central scene of the action. It also introduces the other important character of the story, Mr. Griffin, the geometry teacher. He is probably only a few years older than his students, for the novel mentions that he left the University of Tennessee after only a few years for financial and health reasons. Of course, he becomes a foil for the boy, especially in his relation to the girl. When he asks about a geometrical figure on the board, "she fixed her eyes on him . . . as if to rebuke the creature of straight lines and cold angles for obtruding himself on another world whose lines all curved voluptuously toward some fulfillment he could not possibly understand" (*Circus*, 164–65). This parallels her attitude toward Steve, a younger version of the teacher, who usually answers the questions she cannot.

Embarrassed at his symbolic rejection by the beautiful Helen, the boy looks out the window toward the winter woods where he knows he could walk silently "on the mat of sopping leaves" (*Circus*, 165). Even more intriguing than this escape into nature is the constant imaging of nature as art. The heat of the wood stove in the winter classroom causes the window panes to sweat, "obscuring the printed world" so that "the woods appeared, a depthless misty smudge" (*Circus*, 165). Later in early spring the view of the wet cornfields "was like a print which had been dropped in water so that the splotchy colors ran, merging, and outlines decayed" (*Circus*, 167). Finally, at planting time when the schoolroom windows are opened, "a man followed a plow, seeming in the false perspective rather to ascend the pane than retreat across the field toward the green haze of woods" (*Circus*, 168). Clearly, the boy already sees the world around him, nature and culture, through perspectives provided by the world of art.

In particular, the protagonist reacts in this manner to Helen. With her allusive name, her voluptuous looks, her history of passion, the boy makes her the heroine of his own romantic text. It is not so much one of fulfillment but of rejection, however. For example, he would never get her letter, and she never talks to him at lunch. Rather, the symbolically named Sybil Barnes, "a dark girl, shrewish and bitter," (offers him "devil-food" cake, and comments on "the filthy wart . . . fat and encrusted . . . beside the nail of his finger" (*Circus*, 165–66). At home the boy stands naked in front of his washstand mirror: "In the mirror the hand against the white flesh was gray and clutching like a great spider, the wart monstrous" (*Circus*, 166). This magical, fairy-tale atmosphere makes him into a sort of frog-prince to be saved by the beautiful princess, but she is preoccupied with her demon lover. As one country boy puts it during the first planting of the late spring, "Ain't nobody getting any plowing done . . . 'cept that Frank Barber" (*Circus*, 168).

So when Steve finally rejects Helen and moves beyond her romance, he still must act in terms of artistic texts. Another passage Warren created for the story takes Steve to English class where they are reading Renaissance drama, evidently an autobiographical detail, since Warren has recalled reading Webster's *The White Devil* in his Guthrie high school English class. His textbook quotes from *The Duchess of Malfi*: "*Cover her face: mine eyes dazzle: she died young.*" Reading this line, Steve Adams experiences an epiphany worthy of Joyce's Stephan Daedelus or Wolfe's Eugene Gant: "He felt the veins of the neck throb, and heard, in his ears, the mounting blood that roared, then gradually diminished as when one rides away from the sea" (*Circus*, 169).

When he recovers, he feels "himself far away from her, and much older" (*Circus*, 169), distanced in space and time. He has discovered this ironic distance in art, for in a sense Helen has "died young," lost in her love for the brutish Frank Barber in some strange fulfillment of dysfunctional family patterns. Yet in some way, she is still the princess of the real world; as the story's final line puts it, she "had already . . . inherited the strict and inaccessible province" (*Circus*, 169). In fact, Steve Adam's line of verse obtrudes itself on her as much as Mr. Griffin's straight lines of geometry did earlier. Helen is the reality that the adamic protagonist avoids by creating a negative romance from her short history. We also know from the preceding story that Helen leaves the town, her lover, and her mother and makes her way in the real world. It is not so clear if the academic Steve Adams will prove as successful in making the difficult passage to maturity in the Black Patch or away from it.

"The Confession of Brother Grimes"

"The Confession of Brother Grimes" is the weakest selection in Warren's short-fiction cycle. Although it is readable and amusing, its mordant ironies seem unfocused, especially in terms of its narration. The story's symbolism likewise proves contradictory and manipulated toward an ironic version of an O. Henry surprise ending. Published by the *New English Review* in 1946, the story probably was written about the same time. Certainly, the "smart aleck" narrator seems much in the mode of Jack Burden, the narrator of *All the King's Men*, which appeared in the same year, though without Jack's depth or redemption.[20]

The contrast between the history of Brother Grimes and the narration of that history, evidently made by a cynical member of the preacher's church, creates the central tension of the story. Brother

Grimes, "as good and kind a man as you ever hope to see" (*Circus*, 170), suffers a series of Job-like torments, losing in short order his "stainless" daughter, his "poor" wife, and his "misguided" son-in-law, as well as his own happiness, health, and, perhaps, sanity. Faithful servant of the Lord that he is, the preacher struggles to put these terrible events within the scheme of divine justice. On the other hand, the nameless and faithless narrator relishes the dark humor of the contradictions between culpability and punishment. The breaking of this tension with Brother Grimes's unexpected "confession" ends the narrative in a surprising and somewhat amusing manner, but it hardly resolves the issues raised by the tale or its telling. The "confession" of the title clearly implies both senses of the word, both the preacher's statement of his unwavering faith in God's perfect judgment and his revelation of petty pride.

The events of Brother Grimes's life would try any but the strongest of beliefs, but the preacher is a strong man in every sense. Not only is he a perfect pastor to his flock, a faithful husband to his wife, and a protective father to his daughter, "He always was a fine-looking man, even if he was about sixty-five, a big strong fellow with flashing eyes and a mop of long black hair on his head, not a gray hair in it" (*Circus*, 171). His strong voice and manner match his impressive looks, so he proves a wonderful speaker, as good as William Jennings Bryan on the Cross of Gold, the narrator tells us. This allusion may be important, for Warren lived in Tennessee during the famous Scopes "monkey" trial, the last stand of the Great Commoner against the tide of Darwinism, modernism, and secularism. Like Bryan, Brother Grimes seems a fine man who has outlived his era and is incapable of meaningful change. The preacher's particular preoccupation is God's perfect justice, an idea he touches in every sermon.

As the doubting narrator puts it, the Lord fits the punishment to the crime. Then he speculates on the cause of all the sorrows heaped on the poor preacher. In his age, after a decade as pastor in the town, his daughter, Sue, marries the local wastrel, Archie Munn. Archie is a "ne'er do well" on the model of Alec Nabb in "A Christian Education," a story with which this one seems to pair meaningfully. "He was a likker head, and no woman who valued her reputation . . . would be caught out with him, and no man who wanted to stay out of the hospital would ride in a car with him" (*Circus*, 171); or, in more smart-alecky terms, "He was God's gift to dealers in spiritous likkers, Henry Ford, and the medical profession" (*Circus*, 171). Surely he is not God's gift to Brother Grimes, but his cross to bear.

Only six months after their sudden marriage, Archie kills his new wife in a drunken highway accident. However, the narrator reduces this tragedy to black humor: "The truck had a pole sticking out behind, and it went through that Ford, including Sue Grimes Munn, like a tooth pick through a club sandwich" (*Circus*, 170). In short order, Mrs. Grimes dies of a broken heart, or, as the narrator puts it, ". . . her heart never having been any good to speak of anyway, and you might add her liver-and-lights for that matter" (*Circus*, 170). Archie Munn is physically, if not mentally, broken up by the accident "with so many bones sticking out of him he looked like a mad porcupine" (*Circus*, 170). Therefore, the narrator concludes, "The punishment was pretty general, not to mention a nigger on top the truck who got thrown off and skidded on the place where some people claimed his face had been" (*Circus*, 171).

After each of these tragedies, Brother Grimes struggles back into the pulpit to labor at making them fit into his idea of God's perfect justice. The smirking narrator, evidently one of the preacher's auditors in the congregation, ironically comments on how none of the poor souls involved deserved any of this, with the possible exception of Archie. After his daughter's death, Brother Grimes is pale and shaken; after his wife's death, his hair turns "white as snow" (*Circus*, 173). Later Archie returns from the hospital to live with his father-in-law, and Brother Grimes celebrates God's justice in the return of this prodigal. Then true to his fallen nature, Archie "threw that crutch away, got hold of some whiskey and a car, and went out and killed two white men and a horse in broad daylight" (*Circus*, 173). Archie, like Alec Nabb and Little Jebb, is put in the penitentiary. In a last effort to find a cause for all his sorrow, Brother Grimes makes his confession of "pride and sinful vanity" (*Circus*, 174) which brought this fall. As the narrator's last, ironic sentence states: "He had, he said, used black hair dye for twenty years" (*Circus*, 174).

Although this surprising twist may prove amusing at first reading, its symbolism and irony do not create a focus for the story. Either the poor preacher has become addled by his terrible experiences, in which case the narrator's ironies seem pointlessly cruel, or the confession is "truthful," in which case these same ironies seem pointlessly trivial. In the final analysis the careful reader is not quite sure of how to take the concluding revelation. Unlike the coda in "Blackberry Winter," for example, the ambivalence of viewpoints in the story creates no meaningful ambiguity. In the most basic terms, the two meanings of his confession—the faith and the revelation—neither cohere nor find symbolic tension. Rather, the story seems an exercise in point of view and symbolic incident which simply does not succeed. Comparison with another ironic questioning of traditional faith, "A Christian Education," will demonstrate how "The Confession of Brother Grimes" falls short.

"Her Own People"

"Her Own People" is one of the most intriguing stories in Warren's short-fiction cycle, though it is also a singular effort that has little connection with any of the other stories in Warren's collection.[21] First published by the *Virginia Quarterly Review* in 1935, the story seems to derive from the writer's years on the faculty at Vanderbilt. The central characters are a young white couple, the Allens. Bill Allen is a journalist in the lackadaisically muckraking tradition of Jack Burden; he spends his time at home either writing or partying, leaving the domestic duties to his wife, Annabelle. The Allens live in an old country house outside a small city somewhere in Tennessee, perhaps Nashville. Both Allens find support for their exurban life-style from their black neighbors Jake and Josie, as well as their cook, Viola, whom they have taken away from "her own people" in Alabama. The story differs from the others set in Warren country because it centers on young exurban professionals and, more importantly, the complicated, almost peculiar, relationships between the races in the Upper South.

Race is a factor in all the stories, an issue in several of them, and even an important issue in a few, notably "Blackberry Winter." More often than not racial relations provide an important index to moral positions and developments on the part of the white characters, especially the narrators. White characters or narrators who use the word "Negro," the polite usage for blacks at the time Warren was writing, are generally good people willing to relate to others without prejudice or exploitation; those who use the more common "nigger" are less well developed people, morally and/or socially; while the characters and narrators who employ racial slurs and stereotypes are invariably the least developed and reliable. Yet in only a few stories does this indexing provide an important focus. "Blackberry Winter" is the most obvious example, when the black family provides a chiaroscuro contrast with the white family. The stories that derive from Warren's rural background at his grandfather's farm—"When the Light Gets Green" and "Prime Leaf"—use black tenant families in much the manner, though without the fuller portraits, of "Blackberry Winter."

Warren's attitudes toward race undoubtedly developed from his background as a border southerner born near the turn of the twentieth century. Although his world was marked by racial segregation and prejudice—as was most of America at that time—he did not experience the apartheidlike caste system of Faulkner's Mississippi or other parts of the deeper South. This difference in attitude can be explained by both the smaller black population and by the relative political enlightment of the Upper South. Warren mentions several times in his reminiscences that his own family was liberal in political, religious, and racial attitudes. His grandfathers who rode with Forrest were personally opposed to slavery, and his father neither used himself nor allowed the word "nigger" to be used in his presence. Although Warren is often associated with the somewhat reactionary racial positions of the Fugitive-Agrarians, his own attitudes quickly changed. His essay on race, "The Briar Patch" in *I'll Take My Stand* (1930) is segregationist but not racist; in fact, the editors thought about rejecting Warren's contribution as too liberal. The author has also remarked how his return to the South from England (where "The Briar Patch" was written) during the depths of the Depression quickly changed his outlook (*Talking*, 383–85). We can trace these changes in works of both fiction and nonfiction, including his later studies of the race question, *Segregation* and *Who Speaks for the Negro?*

"Her Own People," written in his period of rapid rethinking of racial issues, forms an interesting piece in Warren's mosaic of black and white in southern history. More than any of his other stories, this one focuses directly on race. Specifically, it concerns the symbolic figure of Viola, the young black woman taken away from her own people to become the Allens' cook. Annabelle Allen was attracted to her because she seemed much like herself: neat ("the cleanest nigger I ever saw" [*Circus*, 178]), slender, lightly complected, and stylish. In short, as Bill Allen puts it, "Viola is a white-folks' nigger" (*Circus*, 178). As in "Blackberry Winter," this phrase is used to cover a multitude of social sins, but unlike the narrator in that story, Bill is unconscious of the irony in his expression. He is paid "to dish political dirt for the *Advocate*" (*Circus*, 176), but he is too blind to recognize the central political contradiction of his region: racial segregation. His wife, though personally more kindly, exhibits the same patronizing obtuseness toward Viola. In short, she expects Viola to be happy as a lesser version of herself, a sort of Cinderella sister surrogate. Viola can do the dirty work of Annabelle's domestic arrangement, wear Annabelle's hand-me-down clothes, and accept Annabelle's dollar-a-day wages with "thankfulness" (*Circus*, 185). No wonder they have, as Annabelle puts it, constant "lover's quarrels" (*Circus*, 177).

This pattern of exploitation of blacks by whites is complicated by the neighboring black couple, Jake and Josie, who are exploited by the Allens, but who in turn exploit the homeless Viola by taking half her wages for room and board. The older, and literally darker, couple seem both attracted to and resentful of Viola's closer relationship with the white couple. In fact, they have the first falling out with the stranger, which Annabelle attributes to Josie's sexual jealousy. Her interpretation suggests the issue may be at least subconsciously present in the white woman's mind as well, a fear that Viola might prove her domestic surrogate in more ways than she intends. In any case, the black couple prove no more Viola's "own people" than do the exploiting Allens.

In some sense, Viola is a later-day version of the "tragic mulatto" of nineteenth-century southern romance, a type Warren considered more fully in the person of Amantha Starr in *Band of Angels*. As in his later historical novel, Warren employs the romance of southern history in this story to contrast with the harsh realities of racial relations in the Depression South. Viola neither fits in the world of whites nor blacks, not socially or even physically. The immediate cause of the falling out that forms the plot of the story is Viola's reactive manipulation of both couples to buy a new outfit she admires more than Annabelle's hand-me-downs. Viola says, "I seed a girl one time outer my winder and she had on a gray dress and gray shoes and a gray coat and hat . . . all gray" (*Circus*, 183).

In essence, Viola is asserting her singular identity between the worlds of white and black, an assertion that neither the white nor the black couple understands at all. In fact, Bill's sarcasm, intended to be at Viola's expense, reveals his own lack of insight or understanding. When Annabelle complains about Viola's spending her savings, he smirks: "Just like the good book says, 'Man does not live by bread alone'" (*Circus*, 182). And later he adds, "that nigger's got a sense of values . . . my little philanthropist" (*Circus*, 182). Of course, at a deeper level than he intends, Bill is perfectly correct: Viola does need more from the white couple than their philanthropy, and more from the black couple than room and board. Jake's self-righteous comments are almost as ironic: "But she ain't my wife's and my kind of people" (*Circus*, 181).

In the end, both couples conspire to send Viola back to "her own people" (*Circus*, 186). However, she refuses to go, even after being fired by Annabelle and ordered out by Josie. She stays in her little room, dressed in her gray outfit, living on cheese and crackers. She has become a sort of mulatto Bartleby, a despondent victim of the culture who refuses to disappear conveniently. As at the end of Melville's famous story, the cultural castoff affects even the most obtuse. Both couples are "fed up" (*Circus*, 189), but the blacks are at least "worrit" (*Circus*, 189) and the whites pitying. Still, neither couple recognizes that they are really Viola's "own people." In this morally bankrupt insistence that they have no responsibility toward their symbolic sister, the story also recalls Faulkner's famous tale of almost exactly the same period, "That Evening Sun" (1931). A comparison of the two works, with their carefully observed characters, subtle plots, symbolic settings, and images of dark and light, demonstrates that Warren's unheralded story proves almost as effective as Faulkner's much more famous tale.

"The Life and Work of Professor Roy Millen"

If "Her Own People" seems to stand by itself, a condition emphasized by its changed position in Warren's final arrangement of his short-fiction cycle, the next two stories, "The Life and Work of Professor Roy Millen" and "The Unvexed Isles," are definitely paired. The most obvious connections arise from subject matter, for both are academic stories—hardly surprising since their author was a full-time academic during the entire period in which he was writing short fiction. Given the similar subject matter of the stories, other parallels follow in terms of characters (professors and students), plots (mutual betrayals by mentors and protégés), and settings (colleges and their environs). Although his academic stories demonstrate themes similar to the tales set in the Black Patch, especially variants on the Freudian family romance, these stories have a different, less realized feel than the other pieces in his collection, and they ultimately prove considerably weaker in quality. Academic fiction overall tends toward banality because perhaps, as the old maxim on academic politics has it, "the stakes are so small." Only a few modern American academic fictionists such as

Lionel Trilling, Randall Jarrell, and John Updike have succeeded with these materials. Although Robert Penn Warren was an accomplished academic and a first-rate fictional writer, his academic fiction must be judged rather forgetable, except for its oblique commentary on his personal and professional life, his career and canon, his life and work.[22]

The first of the pair, "The Life and Work of Professor Roy Millen," rests on just such a dichotomy. Like many academic stories, it ironically contrasts the sort of professional biography that might appear on a resume or in an academic directory with the psychological tensions of an actual life. In both these stories this contrast is best seen through the tensions of academic marriage that shape the professors' lives and works. In turn, these childless marriages seek completion in teacher-student relations that turn sour in dramatized scenes directly out of the pattern of family romance. In these stories, however, the symbolism seems a bit obvious and the plots are forced toward surprise endings found in Warren's weaker works of short fiction, like "The Confession of Brother Grimes."

Professor Roy Millen began his life as what would be poor white trash in the other stories. Perhaps his home country is outside the Black Patch, but his earliest recollection is of picking cotton, "with the sun bearing down on his shoulders and the humid air swimming around him" (*Circus*, 191). In succeeding years he clerks in crossroads stores and teaches in one-room country schools. Later he manages to attain a scholarship to a small denominational college, a doctorate in English, and finally an instructorship at the state university as a replacement for a regular instructor on medical leave.

The shaping force in his career, however, is his wife, born Mildred Saunders, the daughter of the legendary English department head at the university. When Roy met her, he was 39, while "She was a tallish woman, a little past thirty, with a spindly figure and plain features" (*Circus*, 192). Quiet and shy, but kindly, Mildred encourages the young instructor's attentions, and he has the sense to marry her. A regular instructorship soon follows, and in succeeding years timely promotions to a tenured full-professorship, along with other appropriate rewards, material and psychological.

The story itself dramatizes the crisis in his career and his personal life when Mildred dies after a long, lingering illness in the spring of 1937. At first, Professor Millen is understandably lost. He recovers, however, by focusing on his long unfinished *magnum opus*, a book on English literature. Several times the academic couple has been ready to make their trip abroad, to one of "the great English libraries" (*Circus*, 192, 194), in order to finish his project. The last time they were ready to depart, Mildred's health took a turn for the worse, and the trip was diverted to Southern California in hopes that the climate would be good for her health. Of course, California has major libraries, but Professor Millen finds himself caring for his wife, not doing his work. Warren added this amplified Southern California passage to his manuscript, evidently to demonstrate that Professor Millen will never finish his great work, even as a planned "monument" (*Circus*, 193) for Mildred. However, he dutifully plans his trip in June, as soon as he can leave after commencement.

The story's single dramatized scene involves Professor Millen and one of his prize pupils, Tom Howell. The student is rather a stereotyped version of the graduating senior who thinks himself superior to his teachers. At first the professor enthusiastically responds to the young man's request for a recommendation for a postgraduate scholarship to study abroad. However, as young Howell goes on about his opportunities and plans, Roy Millen remembers his own difficult days as a student and comes to resent and reject his protégé. When Howell mentions his two weeks in Paris a few summers earlier, the professor terminates the interview.

The story's final sequence involves three actual texts that occupy the professor's attention for the afternoon, as well as another—the incomplete great book—that rounds out the overall symbolism of the scene. First, Tom leaves the circular describing the scholarship; the older man "read it again, very carefully, dwelling on it almost painfully, as though he was an illiterate trying to extract some secret from the words" (*Circus*, 197). All he can hear is "the boy . . . saying, 'you know how Paris is, it sort of knocks you off your feet'" (*Circus*, 197). Of course, Roy Millen has never been to Paris. Although he starts one very positive recommendation for Mr. Howell, he destroys it and pens a more subtly phrased letter, obviously intended to do his protégé out of the scholarship. This one he signs "Roy Millen, *Professor of English*" (*Circus*, 197; emphasis Warren's), blots, seals, stamps, and mails.

Even in summary, the story's defects are obvious. Both the narrative and the symbolism seem rather obvious and pat. Beyond that problem, the dramatized incident, the betrayal of young Howell, seems only obliquely connected to the central tensions of Professor Millen's life. Although the story suggests a parallel between the young man's brief career and the professor's longer commitment, the central connection is between the student and the work, or more precisely between the two unsuccessfully connected texts: the great work and the letter of recommendation. However, the story provides neither enough detail or focus to make this comparison really effective enough to create a successful tale.

"The Unvexed Isles"

A parallel story; "The Unvexed Isles" provides more detail and a more complex symbolic focus, yet the same problems of typed characters, obvious plots, and unrealized settings finally limit its success as well. In this version of academe, the professorial type is George Dalrymple, the son of a Nebraska dirt farmer, who has lifted himself, by dint of hard work much like Roy Millen, to a tenured professorship at a liberal arts college in Russell Hill, Illinois. His career, as well as personal development, has been advanced by his marriage to the former Alice Bogan of Baltimore, a Junior Leaguer and sentimental poet, willing to settle for a professor with little prospect for advancement. From an affluent background, she finds life at 429 Poplar Street in Russell Hills disappointing, and she hardly conceals her feelings from her husband. This childless couple seems to develop student protégés as surrogate children, notably Phil Alburt, the scion of a wealthy New York family. As in the preceding story, travel plans on the part of all involved propel the professor toward a realization of his frustrations.

The single dramatized scene in "The Unvexed Isles" is a Sunday night visit by the young Phil to the Dalrymples for drinks during the week just before the Christmas break, evidently during the 1930s. (The story first appeared in the *Magazine* during 1934). All three of the principals have travel plans for the break. Phil is joining his family in Bermuda, much to the envy of both George and Alice. She had planned a visit to Baltimore, but family finances and her hypochondria threaten her plans. George, who has not visited her family in years, actually contemplates returning to Sinking Fork Station in Nebraska, as he tells Phil, "Just a wheat elevator and a siding" (*Circus*, 206). The symbolic intersection of these real and imagined journeys provides the tension of the story.

This tension is soon exacerbated by alcohol. Professor Dalrymple prides himself on serving the best whiskey in Russell Hill. He dispenses his libations carefully: "Sacramentally, the whiskey sloshed in the glass" (*Circus*, 199). George really doesn't care much for whiskey, but he enjoys its symbolism as he pours it in his pantry. It provides him with an imagined connection to a richer, freer, more adventurous life. In fact, the occasion of serving a drink to one of his students is just risqué enough to cause a smile.

However, George is made unpleasantly aware of more striking deviations in Phil's personal behavior. When he hands the boy his drink, he observes the "singular" (*Circus*, 201) fact that Phil's cigarette tips is stained with lipstick. Evidently, his protégé has enjoyed more of the Dalrymples' hospitality than George has realized. To his credit, the professor handles this potentially embarrassing scene with both tact and understanding. He doesn't want to embarrass the student, and he can understand and forgive his wife. George can sympathize with Alice, a tired beauty, who can't even go home for Christmas "Because she married a poor man" (*Circus*, 204). Phil is a symbol for her, as well as for him, of lost youth and hope.

This romantic symbolism is neatly represented through the academic byplay between teacher and student in terms of romantic poetry, the subject of English 40 which they have completed together the previous semester. The professor presents the "best whiskey" in Russell Hill while misquoting Keats's "Ode to a Nightingale": " 'Not the true, the blushing hypocrene . . . but 'twill serve" (*Circus*, 199). It appears the slip is unintentional on the professor's part, but very intentional on Warren's. This becomes more apparent when the student responds more correctly: "It's as much of a beaker full of the warm South as I ask" (*Circus*, 199). When the conversation turns to journeys, and specifically to Bermuda, the professor identifies them as "the happy isles" (*Circus*, 205). They represent everything that is opposite to the prairies of Nebraska or, for the matter, Illinois. After Phil Albert leaves, George kisses Alice and retires to his study to work on "a little Chaucer note" (*Circus*, 204). Instead, he reviews the evening "While the wind sweeping down to great valley of the Mississippi . . . beat on the house" (*Circus*, 210). This last paragraph becomes a final coda contrasting his own sad reality with a romantic image of Phil Alburt riding horseback "down the white beaches beside the blue water of the unvexed isles" (*Circus*, 210).

The romantic image of "the unvexed isles" ends the story with a neat suggestion of the romantic byplay that occured earlier. Of course, Phil Alburt will develop into the same frustrated middle age as the Dalrymples, but the romantic image is important for him as well as for his mentors. This pattern of allusion, along with the other symbolic details and the more meaningful, almost oedipal conflict, make this chronicle of Professor Dalrymple a better story than "The Life and Work of Professor Roy Millen," but it remains a comparatively uninspired effort in comparison to the stories that derive from the writer's past in the Black Patch, stories like "Prime Leaf," which concludes the volume.

"Prime Leaf"

As I mentioned at the outset of this study, the author's "Note" that introduces *The Circus in the Attic and Other Stories* (1947), "The earliest story in this book was written in 1930, the latest in 1946, but the order is not chronological," can be read in several ways. Warren probably intends the chronological order of composition here, but other chronologies involving historical and/or fictional time are suggested as well. In fact, Warren seems to reverse the order of his composition by placing his "first piece of fiction," the novella "Prime Leaf," at the conclusion of his collection. Although his arrangement was undoubtedly influenced by a need to balance the title novella's initial position, Warren also intended to emphasize "Prime Leaf" through final placement. Although in its title and text "The Circus in the Attic" metaphorically encapsulates the author's achievements at mid career, "Prime Leaf" announces the writer's primary commitments to his literary heritage in both its title and text. As we have seen, Warren's romance of southern history is a "circus in the attic," or a creative dialectic between imagination and memory. "Prime Leaf" suggests not only Warren's "own peculiar province," the Black Patch of Kentucky and Tennessee, but his own primal narrative, his version of the southern family romance.

Again, we have seen how the titles of all of Warren's short pieces are important to their themes, and this proves true particularly of the titles of the novellas that bracket his short-fiction cycle. The phrase "Prime Leaf" works on several levels of meaning. First, it provides a representative detail in the novella's realistic depiction of the historical Tobacco wars fought during the first decade of this century. The Black Patch along the western borderlands of Kentucky and Tennessee is the home of dark-fired tobacco, so called because its dark green leaf becomes even darker when cured with wood smoke. Some of its growers banded together against the "tobacco trusts," especially the Dukes' American Tobacco Company. These embattled farmers believed the trusts were forcing down the price of their produce, especially of "prime leaf," or the finest grade of tobacco leaf. Between

1907 and 1911 various attempts were made by the tobacco growers to boycott the trusts and drive up the price for their product. Unfortunately, it proved much easier for a few tobacco manufacturers to organize than for thousands of farmers, especially since most of the farmers depended on tobacco as their only cash crop. The regional tradition of independence and individuality further complicated organization, and soon the associated growers were ranged against not just the trusts but nonassociated growers, called "Hillbillies" because they farmed the less productive ridges and knobs of the region. Threats, coercion, and violence soon followed, quickly erupting into a small civil war, in which towns and trains were seized, barns and warehouses burned, and many partisans on both sides injured or killed.

Born in 1905, Robert Penn Warren was only a very small child during the Tobacco wars, but he grew up with the legends of this recent conflict, legends that marked his region as much as the War between the States. As the author remarked as recently as 1978, "It seems to me that all your vital images are ones you get before you're seven, eight, nine years old" (*Talking*, 331). In the same interview Warren insisted on the importance of place in his work, of region, even of province. Of course, Warren was most taken with other writers, particularly his historical forebears, endowed with a unique sense of place. In his masterful essay on Nathanial Hawthorne, Warren discusses how the right relationship to region, to the historical New England he calls the romancer's "own peculiar province," fueled Hawthorne's particular genius. So Warren's own creativity was rooted in his native soil, his fatherland, his *patria*. He would return to it throughout his career, from his first fictions to his last poetry and prose reminiscence, for example, *Portrait of a Father* (1988).

Warren would recycle the subject matter of "Prime Leaf," the Tobacco wars, in his first published novel, *Night Rider* (1939). As several Warren scholars have recognized, the novella provides the matrix of the novel in terms not just of geographical and chronological setting, but also of character and plot, theme and symbol. Indeed, most of the criticism on "Prime Leaf" has been most concerned with how it became *Night Rider*. However, several critics, notably Allen Shepherd, have remarked how the novella has many strengths not discovered in the novel, though *Night Rider* is obviously more complexly developed.[23] Warren's careful research for the novel, which included a trip to the Black Patch and reading both primary and secondary sources, demonstrates his commitment to the material and to a just treatment of it. Finally, *Night Rider* fulfills the definition of the historical novel that Warren develops at the conclusion of the Hawthorne essay, even as he insists his book is not an historical effort.

Warren wrote "Prime Leaf" during his stay as a Rhodes Scholar at Oxford, far from the Black Patch and historical sources, either oral or written. The author has commented several times on the importance of this first creative experience with fiction to his later development. Asked for a contribution to the new journal *American Caravan* by one of its editors, Paul Rosenfeld, Warren responded with several poems, from which the editors chose "Tryst on Vinegar Hill," an earthy piece about a black couple making love in a cemetery near a barely disguised Guthrie, Kentucky. When Rosenfeld inquired about fiction, Warren turned the legends of the Tobacco wars into a novella. Warren remembered, "Fiction was for me a way of reliving a life I was separate from" (*Talking*, 33). In other words, Warren created not historical fiction, but historical romance, as he defines it in the Hawthorne essay: "But the writer of romance would use the actualities of the past as a means of validating and generalizing the moral psychological drama. . . . *the writer of the romance aims at converting the past into a myth for the present*" ("Hawthorne," 459).

This sense of myth and romance, of legend and tale suggests other readings of Warren's title, "Prime Leaf"; although the phrase becomes an important realistic detail in the novella, appearing four times in this context, it also must reflect some awareness on its author's part of the primary commitments represented in his first fiction. By contrast, the title *Night Rider* suggests a realistic detail, but one of more historical and social concern. "Prime Leaf" puts its emphasis on nature itself, on the agricultural product that forms the very matrix of the region's culture. The movements of the seasons, as well as the rhythms of life, are measured in the cycle of tobacco: planting, topping, gathering, curing, marketing. Even the cold wet winters provide the time to rest workers and animals, to repair gear and structures, and to nurture seedlings to renew the process in the spring. We can see signs of this primary importance of tobacco in other stories of the Black Patch—"Blackberry Winter" and "When the Light Gets Green"—as well as in other works, but it is nowhere more prominent than in "Prime Leaf."

The novella's title also points to the primal cultural unit of Warren's region and his fiction drawn from it: the family. Unlike his novel on the same materials, "Prime Leaf" focuses on a single family, the Hardins, and their reaction to the Tobacco wars. This concentration not only gives the historical developments more human meaning, but it also suggests the immense complexity of the relationship between nature and culture that finds its most significant connection in the family. The Hardins are a farming family, owners of "Cedardale," several hundred acres of well-watered bottom land that produces tobacco and cattle for market. They are also a patriarchal family. The novella centers on the relationships among three generations of Hardin fathers and sons: Joe Hardin, the patriarch; Big Thomas, his son; and Little Thomas, his grandson. Although Cedardale is only a modest farm, it also demonstrates some sense of the plantation family, for the white owners have a paternalistic relationship with a black family substructure. In their relation to this shadow family, as in the relationship of all three men to Edith, Big Thomas's wife and Little Thomas's mother, the family demonstrates the peculiar southern casting of the Freudian family romance remarked by many critics such as Richard King. And, of course, the theme of fathers and fatherland has often been developed by critics of Warren's other works.

Another connection between "Prime Leaf" and Warren's *patria* is the epigraph provided for the original publication of the novella by *American Caravan* in 1931: "*Nec natura potest justo secernere iniquum, Dividit ut bona diversis, fugienda petendis.*" Although Warren does not give a source, it is interesting that it proves to be Horace's *Satires* (1:3:113–14). A literal translation renders these lines as "Nor is nature able to distinguish justice from inequity, in the way that she distinguishes beneficial things from their opposites, things to be avoided from things to be sought." Its context is a comparison of Stoic and Epicurean value systems; for Horace, human good and evil evolves from social contexts, and humankind must develop moral sense, the ability to identify good and evil and to act accordingly, through the process of civilization. Even though the epigraph is omitted from republications of the novella, it provides an excellent introduction to the conflicts of natural, personal, and social morality in "Prime Leaf."

The social conflict in "Prime Leaf" is, of course, the Tobacco wars. The personal conflict concerns the individual in relation to this historical imperative. Warren's own conflicts surface both in the relation of fathers and sons and of whites and blacks. Remember that the writer was only 25 years old when he began "Prime Leaf," at a crucial juncture in terms of the rejection of father figures and the assumption of adult roles in his marriage that same year. Warren has commented not just on the relation of the novella to his home and family, but to the specifics of the racial situation that he had left behind in the American South. At the same time he began "Prime Leaf," he was just finishing "The Briar Patch," his controversial essay on the "race question" which appeared in the Agrarian manifesto *I'll Take My Stand* in 1930. Speaking of his essay, Warren makes this connection himself, "The two things were tied together—the look back home from a long distance" (*Talking*, 33). In its subtle condemnation of segregation and the tenant system, "Prime Leaf" begins Warren's rewriting of the traditions of his fatherland.

"Prime Leaf" proves very accomplished work for the young writer's first effort in fiction. Almost all of its critics give it high praise, even in comparison with more mature work like *Night Rider*. The novella's characters are well realized; its plot compact and seemingly inevitable; its setting well rendered. Perhaps the only problem is point of view. The overall viewpoint is an objective third-person voice that ranges in turn among the perspectives of all the characters but particularly between the oldest and the youngest Hardin males, Old Joe and Little Thomas. Although this view is effective in revealing character, it somewhat diffuses the focus of the work, even as it reveals the relationships of the characters. In particular, it does not put quite enough emphasis on Big Thomas, who should, in a social sense at least, be the central focus of the family structuring.

Just as characterization is focused in the family and its cycle of human life, plot is ordered by the family's relationship to the cycle of the seasons and the resulting stages in the process of producing tobacco for market. For example, "Prime Leaf" opens on a hot Sunday afternoon in August 1907. The Hardins are at their Sunday dinner, with a guest, Mr. Wiedenmeyer, a tobacco buyer. The scene allows Warren to develop several tensions important to his story. The first words are a Protestant grace, evidently pronounced by Big Thomas, which raises the issue of the moral use of nature: "Bless this food to the purposes of our bodies and us to Thy service" (*Circus*, 211). The scene also establishes the symbolic byplay between the members of the family. Grandfather and grandson eye each other incuriously during grace, and Edith turns to her guest "with an appearance of hospitable interest" (*Circus*, 211). Of course, the presence of the tobacco buyer allows the men to begin a discussion of problems with the tobacco business. Also, since the meal is served by Sallie, the black cook, and her son Alec, the racial theme is also introduced. For example, when Alec clatters the dishes, Mrs. Hardin rebukes him gently, but the tobacco buyer remarks, "Shiftless, these niggers, shiftless" (*Circus*, 212). After Mr. Wiedenmeyer leaves, Big Thomas refers to him as "the old Jew" (*Circus*, 225). Both characterizations reflect the prejudices of the region, indeed of a larger America.

The scene shifts to the farmyard when Alec announces that hawks are after their chickens. Old Mr. Hardin still does most of the shooting on the farm and takes Mr. Weidenmeyer outside with him to talk. Of course, the two boys tag along, with Tommy trying to coax his grandfather into letting him have a shot at the hawk. The change of scene indicates how old Joe Hardin in a sense still rules the roost: he still hunts at the age of 69, and he still controls the family business. In fact, he takes the tobacco buyer outside because Big Thomas was becoming irritable during the discussion, and Joe believes he can get more information out of his guest. Their dialogue fills out the picture of the historical situation, while it also characterizes Mr. Hardin as a competent, careful, fair man. The actual shooting prefigures the violence of the novella's conclusion. When the hawk returns, Mr. Hardin allows Tommy a shot, which misses, and then kills the red-tail himself. He draws the analogy for Mr. Weidenmeyer that a man must protect his own. The first part of the novella ends when the tobacco buyer leaves, and the old man retires for a Sunday afternoon nap.

Part 2, which takes place in September after the tobacco is cut, again centers on Mr. Hardin, who has become a director of the tobacco grower's association. Through this section his antagonist is Mr. Hopkins, a hotheaded old friend who has become chairman. Joe Hardin's motivations in terms of the association are complicated and even contradictory. He is a native Carolinian who came to Kentucky after the Civil War, during which he rose to the rank of captain with a battlefield commission. Clearly, he is a successful man and a natural leader; what is more, he seems to want to keep his place in his culture. At the same time, Captain Hardin, as he is still called in the manner of the South, is a genuinely good and thoughtful man, one who is trying to do the right thing for all involved. His pride pushes him into a position that finally becomes untenable.

After the association meeting in the market town of Bardsville, Hardin repairs to the ironically named Utopia Cafe to discuss their cooperative ventures over a drink with Hopkins and Mike Sullivan, a young lawyer who seems the prototype for Perse Munn, the protagonist of *Night Rider*. Their conversation, importantly enough, touches on the relationship of right and law. After the lawyer leaves, Mr. Hopkins reveals that he had been sending threats signed "A Friend" to holdouts from the association. Mr. Hardin allows how this will work in nine of ten cases, but it won't work with all. Bill Hopkins then plays his hole card: if a grower won't scare then he may have to "collect a little insurance" (*Circus*, 235). In other words, his barns would be burned. At this, Joe Hardin warns that he will resign from the board if any more letters are sent and quit the association if any barns are burned. Hopkins asserts his "rights," but Hardin warns him against "some fool farmer who wants his rights" who will shoot him off his horse some night (*Circus*, 237).

At this Hopkins storms out, leaving Joe Hardin to pay for the drinks, eat lunch alone, and kill time in town before the late train to the country. During all this time he worries about the rights and wrongs of the situation. Finally home, he visits the firing barn, where the curing of the tobacco has begun. Again prefiguring the violence of the conclusion, the barns themselves almost seem to be burning. Inside he finds Sam, the black father in the family that includes Sallie and Alec, asleep by the hardwood fire he is supposed to be tending. Like Edith's correction of Alec, Mr. Hardin's rebuke of Sam is mild, but firm. However, he lets Sam go off to bed while he tends the fire, showing both his paternalistic attitude and his worries about his social and moral position.

Part 3 takes place in early winter, the time for selling the tobacco crop. Big Thomas arrives home after an errand with news about nightriders burning and dynamiting barns in the neighborhood. Here the focus seems to be Big Thomas, who in some ways seems in the most difficult position of all. At first, he had no interest in the association, asserting his quick-tempered, independent nature. In this sense, he is more like Mr. Hopkins than his own father, and in some way he seems to be rebelling against the older males who are leading the association. However, after his father took his place on the board, Big Thomas agreed to join. Now, his allegiance is torn between his father, who will quit at this latest news, and his new allies, like Mike Sullivan. As he discusses the situation with Edith, he notes her solicitude for his father, and accuses her of siding with the older Mr. Hardin. Edith Hardin's response is lightly made, but interesting in terms of both her refusal to make a clear choice as well as her imagery: "I do believe you're jealous of your own father. You ought to be spanked like Tommy" (*Circus*, 247).

The scene that follows demonstrates this same interchange of roles between fathers and sons. Old Mr. Hardin has been down to the mailbox to get the afternoon paper, and he returns with little Tommy who has just gotten back from school. All the men are eager to tell their versions of events, and they compete until Tommy is sent to his room. The domestic scene now becomes a triangle, played directly in front of the family hearth. Big Thomas insists that his father will ruin them all, that he wants to keep his hands clean at the expense of others. This image of clean hands, clearly reminiscent of the gospel accounts of Pilate, is repeated several times, as in the line "Just going to call for the bowl and pitcher and wash your hands" (*Circus*, 256). Also Thomas warns that they will all have dirty hands, the males from "grubbing in somebody else's tobacco patch" and Edith from "somebody's dishwater" (*Circus*, 253). It seems ironic that the "ruin" they fear is exactly the lot of their shadow family, the black tenants. Of course, this exchange also gives a moral focus to the economic underpinnings of the tobacco struggles.

When Big Thomas complains that his father always gets his way, the older man agrees to divide the crop and the farm. In fact he goes off to write two letters: one his resignation from the association, the other an offer of his share of the crop to Mr. Wiedermeyer. These letters become interesting texts as J. C. Hardin carefully crosses out the "& Son" from the Cedardale business letterhead. Just as he finishes the letters, Edith comes in bearing a lamp to light the darkening room and the news that Big Thomas has agreed to resign from the association and sell his crop with his father.

Part 4 takes place, symbolically, in deep winter, as the inevitable tragedy ensues. Again it is Edith who seems to be most conscious of the complex realities around her family. She wakes in the middle of the night, suspecting that someone is at the barn. When she wakes Big Thomas, he knows it is nightriders, and he bounds out to the defense, leaving her to waken old Mr. Hardin. By the time the older man reaches the barn it is in full blaze, watched only by the nervous black tenants. Big Thomas has disappeared in pursuit of the nightriders. When the grandfather returns to the farmhouse, he replays the earlier scene before the house with Edith and Tommy, sending them back to bed with a reassuring story that his son has gone to warn the neighbors. Actually, when Big Thomas returns, he confirms his father's fear that he pursued the nightriders. Cutting across the fields, he ambushed them at the main road, shooting the leader from his horse. They in turn chased him, but he escaped by swimming the river and returning to the farm. After a long night's vigil, they get the news that Bill Hopkins was shot, but is expected to recover. In perhaps the most interesting development of this section, Mr. Hardin convinces his son to surrender himself to the sheriff in Bardsville, so that his wife and boy won't see him arrested. Yet when they ride together to the main road, old Mr. Hardin sends him on alone, turning off himself to visit the wounded Mr. Hopkins.

A final short scene switches the focus to young Tommy. He is in school when Sam comes to fetch him; at first "the tall black man" refuses to say why the boy must come home, but as they ride off in the wagon, he stares ahead and tells the boy the truth: "Dey done shot your pappy, son. Dey done killed him down on de pike tow'd town" (*Circus*, 276). A short final paragraph follows that beautifully restates the several themes of the novella. Thus, the seemingly inevitable human tragedy reverses the order of the natural world: spring brings death not life, and the fatherless son is initiated into a fallen world where he will sweat, perhaps, in someone else's tobacco patch. Just as the epigraph from Horace put it, nature does not make moral distinctions, but humankind must make them, difficult as they are in a world of fallen human nature.

The conclusion of "Prime Leaf" is also the final movement in Robert Penn Warren's cycle of short fiction. It can be seen as a perfect endnote, a final punctuation of his universal story. In turn, this failure of fathers forms the basis for the family romance that structures so much of Warren's work, including many of his short fictions. The novella that lends its title to Warren's collection announced this note of the author's "shadowy territory," the romance of southern history. In his "own peculiar province," the Black Patch, Warren re-creates personal and cultural memory through imagination in narratives of several genres and modes. His short fiction, though not as important overall as Warren's work in other genres, provides a central point of focus for his canon and career, an intertextuality that works within this volume and beyond it as well. For this reason, as well as for its narrative quality and accessibility, *The Circus in the Attic and Other Stories* remains, perhaps, the best introduction to modern America's most important man of letters, Robert Penn Warren.[24]

Notes to Part 1

1. Richard B. Sale, "An Interview in New Haven with Robert Penn Warren," in *Talking with Robert Penn Warren*, Floyd C. Watkins, John T. Hiers, and Mary Louise Weaks, eds. (Athens: University of Georgia Press, 1990), 138; hereafter cited parenthetically in the text as *Talking*.

2. "Nathaniel Hawthorne," in *American Literature: The Makers and the Making, 2 vols.*, Cleanth Brooks, R.W.B. Lewis, and Robert Penn Warren, eds. (New York: St. Martins Press, 1973), 2:459; hereafter cited parenthetically in the text as "Hawthorne."

3. Frederic Jameson, "Marxism and Historicism," *New Literary History* 1 (1979): 42.

4. Susan Garland Mann, *The Short Story Cycle: A Genre Comparison and Reference Guide* (Westport, Conn.: Greenwood Press, 1989).

5. These negative critics include Leonard Casper, Charles Bohner, and Allen Shepherd; more positive assessments include those of Marshall Walker, Paul West, and Randolph Runyon. See Part 3 and Bibliography.

6. *The Circus in the Attic and Other Stories* (1947; reprint, New York: Harcourt Brace Jovanovich, Harvest Books, 1975). All page references for the short fiction are to this edition, the most readily available; hereafter cited parenthetically in the text as *Circus*.

7. Joy Bale Boone's "A Circus at the Top," *Louisville Courier-Journal Magazine*, 4 June 1978, pp. 10–15, demonstrates the historical source of Warren's fictional biography in John Wesley Venable, born in 1888 in Hopkinsville, Kentucky, who made a lifelong project of a miniature circus. Venable came to Warren's attention when he revisited the Black Patch during the Depression to research the Tobacco Wars for his first published novel, *Night Rider* (1939). Like Lovehart, Venable was the last branch of an old family, the son of an Episcopal minister and a domineering mother, who resembled Warren's character in many details of his personal and professional life.

However, the geographical and historical background of the novella is modeled on Clarksville, Tennessee, another small city in Warren's Black Patch. The narrator dramatizes its history through four minibiographies: Lem Lovehart, a "long hunter" and founder of Bardsville in 1778; Tolliver Skaggs, another pioneer who built the first brick house in 1811; and Cassius "Cash" Perkins and Seth Sykes, young men killed in the indecisive Battle of Bardsville in December 1861. The point of all these life stories is how the present recycles the past by romanticizing history. The pioneers were really sociopaths unfit for civilization: the first was killed by Indians, the second was a noted Indian killer, and the war "heroes," one a drunk and the other a slacker, were both killed by accident. The present is victimized by the past, for the idealization of these ancestors leads to the phallic votive stone erected during World War I, and it in turn prefigures the patriotic excesses of World War II.

8. Arthur Miller's first important play, *All My Sons*, echoed this theme in the same year, 1947. In a structural sense, the novella also has the feel of modern American drama being written contemporaneously by Thornton Wilder, Tennessee Williams, and Arthur Miller. In turn, the structures of works like *Our Town* (1938), *The Glass Menagerie* (1943), and *The Death of a Salesman* (1949) demonstrate a filmic influence in quick cutting between settings, rapid movement backward and forward across time, and the quick juxtaposition of scene with scene, much as Warren does in his novella. The second-person narration accompanies an opening movement much like a traveling camera shot, leading the reader across the geography of Bardsville into its history.

9. Almost all of the works listed in the Bibliography present positive and insightful readings. Particularly useful readings include those in volumes by Bohner, Casper, Runyon, Walker, and West, as well as the articles by Grubbs, O'Connor, Runyon, Shepherd, Weathers, and Wilhelm.

10. "'Blackberry Winter': A Recollection," in *Understanding Fiction*, 3rd ed. (Englewood Cliffs, NJ: Prentice Hall, 1979), 377; hereafter cited in the text as "Recollection."

11. Of the footprint the narrator goes on to say: "You have never seen a beach, but you have read the book and how the footprint was there" (*Circus*, 64). This possible allusion to *Robinson Crusoe* set up several intertextual reverberations including suggestions of the natural paradise and the confrontation with the "other."

12. For example, see the works by Bohner, Casper, O'Connor, Runyon, Shepherd, Walker, and West.

13. In an interesting detail, both Warren and the narrator hear their grandfathers described as "inveterate" readers, and associate the strange word with their grandfathers' status as Confederate veterans.

14. The story has received very slight critical consideration; most of the general discussions mention it in passing as an effective "anecdote" or "sketch."

15. Several critics discuss the story in these (auto)biographical terms; see Shepherd, Walker, and especially the article in *Mississippi Quarterly* by Will Fridy.

16. Less often reprinted than "Goodwood Comes Back," this story has received less attention from the critics; all of the general studies mention it rather positively, however, especially for its dramatization of agrarian themes.

17. "On 'The Patented Gate and the Mean Hamburger,'" in *On Writing, By Writers*, William W. West, ed. (Boston: Ginn, 1966), 266; hereafter cited parenthetically in the text as "Gate."

18. As one of the slighter selections in the volume, "A Christian Education" has received scant attention.

19. "The Love of Elsie Barton" and "Testament of Flood" are treated by

most critics in terms of the relationship indicated here, but with less consideration of their common source or their patterns of imagery. In particular, see Bohner, Casper, Runyon, Shepherd, Walker, and West.

20. None of the critics has much to say about this story; certainly none argue that it is a success.

21. The story has received remarkably little critical attention considering its important themes and structural neatness.

22. The criticism in general has seen few of these biographical connections and generally has ignored both the academic stories.

23. Although Shepherd's article remains the best development of the connection to the novel, Runyon presents the most complex probing of the novella's imagery. Works with substantial discussion of "Prime Leaf," in addition to Runyon and Shepherd, include Bohner, Casper, O'Connor, Walker, and West.

24. Warren did write a handful of short stories not collected in *The Circus in the Attic*. These include juvenile pieces published in his high school literary magazine, an early unpublished story, "Goodbye Jake," and a short sketch, "Invitation to a Dance," published after his collection. None of these pieces have any important connection with the Black Patch, the short-fiction cycle, or the rest of the Warren cannon. The several pieces of fiction published in journals after 1947 are excised pieces of his later novels.

Part 2

THE WRITER

Introduction

Robert Penn Warren was a respected literary critic as well as a creative writer, and he commented widely, both in interviews and in reminiscent prose, on his own work in all genres. His remarks on short fiction are brief, scattered, and contradictory by comparison to his commentary on his poetry and long fiction. Some of his comments are quoted and analyzed in Part 1, whereas the most representative, extended, and insightful examples are presented here. The "Interview in New Haven" conducted by Richard B. Sale provides a thorough discussion of his short fiction in terms of his models, techniques, and intentions. Warren also wrote fascinating essays on the composition of two of his best-known stories, "Blackberry Winter" and "The Patented Gate and the Mean Hamburger." Both stories were written in 1946, and both commentaries appear to date from the early 1950s; they were first published in 1959 and 1966, respectively.

Interview with Richard B. Sale

Richard B. Sale: Do you have a feeling that some ideas simply suggest themselves as short pieces or poems rather than material for novels? Can you tell pretty well now what you're going to use certain ideas for?

Warren: A poem or a big thing, fiction? Well, short stories are out for me. I haven't written a short story in, now, let's see, since '46. That's twenty-three years. The last two I wrote were my best ones, and I may never do another one. But I discovered that the overlap between the short story and the poem was very bad for me. I didn't finish a single short poem for ten years, from '45—God, it must have been '44 or '45, along in there—until '54. I didn't finish a single short poem, not one. I was working on a long poem during that time, *Brother to Dragons*, but I didn't finish it then. I must have started fifty short poems. Not one panned out. I threw them all away, and some of them were going okay. I couldn't finish them; they died on me. For ten years every one of them died. Which is all to the good!

During that period I reassessed my whole feeling about the question you were asking me. I began to see that I had, in a way, too abstract a view of what constituted the germ of a poem *for me*. I mean that when I went back to writing short poems, the poems were more directly tied to a realistic base of facts. They're more tied up with an event, an anecdote, an observation, you see. They were closer to me, closer to my observed and felt life. They had literal germs. That doesn't mean they were autobiographical in the rigid sense of the word. But they were tied more directly to the sort of thing that might become a short story. And once this sense of using such material for poems became clear, I said, "I don't want to write another short story." It was killed just like that. I'd never write short stories again. I just didn't want to

Richard B. Sale conducted this interview in 1969; it was published in *Studies In The Novel*, 11 (Fall 1970): 325–54. Copyright © 1970 by North Texas University. Excerpted and reprinted by permission of the publisher.

have any more to do with them. They felt cramping to me, and I just didn't want to fool with them any more. Happy I was to quit. But this decision somehow seemed to be related to the notion of a poem that is tied closer to the texture of casual life, incidental life, incidental observation, direct experience. There's that. They moved into that world, poetry did. So most of the short poems—that is, many, many, many since then—could very easily have turned at one point into a short story.

Sale: But now poetry has come to take the place of the short story.

Warren: That's it, that's right. When I wrote the last two short stories, I really liked them. I've only liked three or so that I've written—maybe four at the most. I was thinking the best at the very end, and I suddenly got nauseated with the whole idea of doing short stories or novelettes. And there it was. The poems and a complete change of attitude toward what constituted the germ of a short poem happened in that period. . . .

Sale: You mentioned several writers just in passing at different times. What of your early interest in other writers, in Faulkner, say. When did you first come across William Faulkner's works, do you recall?

Warren: Exactly. Every detail of it. When I was a student at Oxford, I knew John Gould Fletcher in London, and John Gould Fletcher came up to Oxford for a weekend visit with me and brought me several books as presents. One was Hart Crane's *The Bridge* in the Black Paris edition, and one was MacLeish's *New Found Land* in the Black Paris edition and one was *Soldiers' Pay*, just out in England. He gave me this book and said, "You want to read *Soldiers' Pay*. It's wonderful writing. You'd better read it right quick." I read it and I remember on the back it had a blurb by Arnold Bennett which said, "An American who writes like an angel."

Sale: That's one of those generation bridges you were talking about before.

Warren: That certainly is one of them and how ironical that one is. And I read the book and I thought it was just great. Of course it's not great but it set well. What was wonderful about it was the scene in that book—a certain shock of recognition to see a certain aspect of the South that you were aware of but never formulated. I'm not a Mississippian, but somehow there's enough generalized South for this to be interesting and important to me, and I read it at a time when I

85

was starting to write. I'd already started my first novel, and my first piece of fiction was being published: *Prime Leaf*. I was writing it at the request of Paul Rosenfeld for *The American Caravan*. He'd asked me to do a piece of fiction along the line of the tales we've been talking about. I was living back into my South, and here comes a novel about the South bringing a real shock of recognition. This hit me at the moment when I was puzzling with the question of what to do with Southern tales. And Katherine Anne Porter's tales about the South had been very important to me and so had Caroline Gordon's and some others. I got to know some fiction writers, you see. They talked about fiction the way I'd always heard poetry talked about.

Sale: With the same excitement.

Warren: Same excitement, same sense of being a complicated, rich thing inside. You know about it. That's the excitement they brought to it.

Sale: When you were at L.S.U. in 1934, was Faulkner a popular author there?

Warren: Well, again, I read him. I read the short stories when they came out and was mad for them. I read all the books when they came out. Yes—I, and all of my friends were this way, my historian friends were. Yes, the people who were interested in history had a passionate devotion to his work. I don't mean uncritical devotion, but a passionate interest in it. People had read him there. I felt I'd discovered him, but everybody I know practically had discovered him.

Sale: I guess a lot of people had privately discovered him.

Warren: A lot, yes. Well, you know a few years later you couldn't find one of his books. I've recently read all, practically all, the reviews of Faulkner from 1929 to 1941.

Sale: And it didn't take too long.

Warren: Incredibly, to the whole Marxist school, he was the Southern fascist. They polished him off.

Sale: Not to be read.

Warren: It's incredible. It's one of the saddest, most humbling and distressing pieces of intellectual history I know. About then *Strange Fruit* came out. You had a pack and chorus, even being led by the Roosevelt administration, of praise for that book. And what a cocky book. *Go Down, Moses* came out then, too. "The Bear" was in it.

Nobody mentioned it. That book died a-borning. And *Strange Fruit* was a great big thing.[1]

Sale: Yes, it was.

Warren: Now, after that you couldn't buy a work of Faulkner's. They were all out of print. There were a few paperbacks floating around, but you couldn't get one through a regular channel.

Sale: You could in England, but you couldn't in the United States.

Warren: You could in Italy. . . .

Sale: Oh, about Katherine Anne Porter. Have you got any comment to make about where *Ship of Fools* fits into the total work?

Warren: I don't—Let's see. *Ship of Fools* is a big, important book, but I think its powers are powers of a series of novelettes imbedded in it. I couldn't put the book down when I read it. I read it right straight through in two solid days of reading. Didn't get out of my chair [but] to eat and go to bed. It is faulty, but I was expecting it; the end is not the end of a novel. You've had some wonderful novelettes on the way, I think. This is nothing against it. I say it's nothing against her. She's a terrific writer. Of the world's best twenty novelettes, she might probably have two of them. They're really great. I mean they're at the world level, you know. I would think "Old Mortality" and "Noon Wine" or maybe "Pale Horse" would be at the top level, you know, in that collection of the world's short novels. She would have one or two. She's bound to have one. She may have two in there. And several short stories are absolutely first rate. I'm not talking about wonderful; I'm talking about really the first-rate ones, you know. She's a terrific writer. She's natural for it. She has a genius for short fiction. The amount of density, of philosophical density, the human weight that she can get into things like "Old Mortality"! It's as big as a big novel. Or what she could get into "Noon Wine."

Sale: Or—what's the phrase?—to *get away with* having that much in it.

Warren: That's right, that's right.

Sale: To get away with it, not just packing it in.

Warren: Having it there, having it totally absorbed in its own scale. The resonance and the drama and the echoes of it. This is terrific. Now, I don't think about her personally. She's one of my oldest and dearest friends, and I don't think this is just friendship making me say this. But she has this power of getting these ranges of meaning into the short form. I think these same powers are in *Ship of Fools*, but not as a *novel*, not in *Ship of Fools* as novel, but in elements of *Ship of Fools*. They're not digested in the novel, they're not digested. But the novel, the novel thing does not hold all that's in that novel.

Sale: Would you put Eudora Welty in her category?

Warren: I think Eudora is a terrific writer. I'll say that, yes, I think Eudora's best stories are in the top level. There are not many first-rate short-story writers, not many natural short-fiction writers. Eudora's one of them. In this country, how many do we have, really? We've had—Faulkner. He's had several short stories and "The Bear" which are top level. Katherine Anne, Eudora Welty, Hemingway. Fitzgerald has a couple of them, I think, that are real beauties. The rather long one called "Winter Dreams" is a beauty and "Rich Boy" is gratifying. And then you begin to thin out fast, you know. You begin to grope around. Now, you will find many fine stories, men of two or three stories.

Sale: Single stories.

Warren: A single story or maybe two by somebody who's a novelist. There's a wonderful story by John Peale Bishop, quite a wonderful story. Caroline Gordon has two beautiful stories. Let's see—John O'Hara, now, he is a short-story writer. The same kind Moravia is or that Pirandello was. The same kind that Chekhov was or de Maupassant. He pours them out. Just pours them out automatically. And the problem is reading him. I've come rather lately to this view, but I got to reading a lot of them in a great run when I was in France last year just because they were available there in paperback. I was detached from them so far, I began to see that some of these are quite wonderful. But you have to read ten to find the good one. This is the way with de Maupassant. He's a very great writer, I think. He's much out of fashion now. He also was a fine novelist. And Pirandello or Moravia, but you have to read through so many to find that one because the good ones look like the bad ones. And the bad ones are so well turned out. They are so close to the good ones, don't you see. You have to take three or four looks to see the difference. And I've come to think that John O'Hara is really a superlative short-story writer. I think you have to look, try to see the bad from the good, the almost good from the really good, but there's some quite powerful things he's done. He's a natural. He's a natural-born story writer; anyway, I think he's underrated.

There are two or three novels that really matter, but he's also a real short-story writer.

Oh, I also wanted to record my admiration for Flannery O'Connor. I would put her name in that same group of the best short-fiction writers. She's written some beauties, much better than her novels.

Sale: Did you know her?

Warren: I knew her slightly. I spent one weekend as a guest in the same house with her. That's the only time I ever saw her, in Nashville. She was a fascinating woman, wonderful writer. The short-story psychology is a strange, strange thing. It's as different from a novel in a way as poetry is. Well, not quite, but there's a real difference. She was a wonderful writer. She's going to be permanent, I think.

Sale: Yes.

Warren: Well, Peter Taylor's done some excellent short stories.

Sale: Okay, one more writer. How does Hemingway wear on you, looking back?

Warren: Very well indeed, I think. In my fiction class here I use Hemingway, and now nobody's read him. The students haven't read him. Five years ago everybody read him. Now they have not and they don't even want to because he's dead.

Note

1. *Go Down, Moses* was published in the spring of 1942 and had been out for two years when the novel by Lillian Smith appeared.

"Blackberry Winter": A Recollection

I remember with peculiar distinctness the writing of this story, especially the balance, tension, interplay—or what you will—between a sense of compulsion, a sense that the story was writing itself, and the flashes of self-consciousness and self-criticism. I suppose that in all attempts at writing there is some such balance, or oscillation, but here the distinction between the two aspects of the process was peculiarly marked, between the ease and the difficulty, between the elation and, I am tempted to say, the pain. But the pain, strangely enough, seemed to be attached to the compulsion, as though in some way I did not want to go into that remembered world, and the elation attached to the critical effort I had to make to ride herd on the wrangle of things that came milling into my head. Or perhaps the truth is that the process was more complicated than that and I shall never know the truth, even in the limited, provisional way the knowing of truth is possible in such matters.

It crosses my mind that the vividness with which I have always remembered the writing of this story may have something to do with the situation in which it was written. It was the fall or winter of 1945–46 just after the war, and even if one had had no hand in the blood-letting, there was the sense that the world, and one's own life, would never be the same again. I was then reading Herman Melville's poetry, and remember being profoundly impressed by "The Conflict of Convictions," a poem about the coming of the American Civil War. Whatever the rights and wrongs of the matter, the war, Melville said, would show "the slimed foundations" of the world. There was the sense in 1945, even with victory, that we had seen the slimed foundations, and as I now write this, the image that comes into my mind is the homely one from my story—the trash washed by the storm from under Dellie's cabin to foul her pridefully clean yard. And I should not be surprised

Reprinted from Cleanth Brooks and Robert Penn Warren, *Understanding Fiction*, 3rd ed. (Englewood Cliffs, NJ: Prentice Hall, 1979), 377–82. © 1979. Reprinted by permission of the publisher.

if the picture in the story had its roots in the line from Melville as well as in such a fact, seen a hundred times in my rural boyhood. So the mixed feelings I had in our moment of victory in 1945, Melville's poem, and not only the image of Dellie's cabin, but something of the whole import of my little story, belong, it seems, in the same package.

For a less remote background, I had just finished two long pieces of work, a novel called *All the King's Men* and a critical study of Coleridge's poem *The Ancient Mariner*, both of which had been on my mind for years. Both those things were impersonal, about as impersonal as the work of any man's hand can be said to be. Even though much of my personal feeling had been drawn into both projects, they belonged to worlds very different from my own. At that time, too, I was living in a very cramped apartment over a garage, in a big, modern, blizzard-bit northern city, again a place very different from the world of my story.

In my daily life, I certainly was not thinking about and remembering that world. I suppose I was living in some anxiety about the fate of the two forthcoming pieces of work, on which I had staked much, and in the unspoken, even denied, conviction that some sort of watershed of life and experience was being approached. For one thing, the fortieth birthday, lately passed, and the sense of let-down after the long period of intense work, could account, in part at least, for that feeling.

Out of this situation the story began, but it began by a kind of accident. Some years earlier, I had written a story about a Tennessee sharecropper, a bad story that had never been published. Now I thought I saw a way to improve it. I don't know whether I actually sat down to rewrite the story that was to have the new avatar of "The Patented Gate and the Mean Hamburger," or whether I got side-tracked into "Blackberry Winter" first. In any case, I was going back into a primal world of recollection. I was fleeing, if you wish. Hunting old bearings and benchmarks, if you wish. Trying to make a fresh start, if you wish. Whatever people do in their doubleness of living in a present and a past.

I recollect the particular thread that led me back into that past: the feeling you have when, after vacation begins, you are allowed to go barefoot. Not that I ever liked to go barefoot, not with my bony feet. But the privilege itself was important, a declaration of independence from the tyranny of winter and school and, even, your own family. It was like what the anthropologists call a rite of passage. But it had another meaning, too. It carried you back into a dream of nature, the woods not the house was now your natural habitat, the stream not the street. Looking out into the snow-banked alley of that iron latitude where I now lived, I had a vague, nostalgic feeling and wondered if spring would ever come. (It finally came—and then on May 5 there was again snow, and the heavy-headed blooms of lilac were beautiful with their hoods of snow and beards of ice.)

With the recollection of going barefoot came another, which had been recurrent over the years: the childhood feeling of betrayal when early summer gets turned upside-down, and all its promises are revoked by the cold-spell, the gully-washer. So by putting those two recollections together, the story got started. I had no idea where it was going, if anywhere. Sitting at the typewriter was merely a way of indulging nostalgia. But something has to happen in a story, if there is to be more than a dreary lyric poem posing as a story to promote the cause of universal boredom and deliquescent prose. Something had to happen, and the simplest thing ever to have happen is to say: *Enter, mysterious stranger.* And so he did.

The tramp who thus walked into the story had been waiting a long time in the wings of my imagination—an image drawn, no doubt, from a dozen unremembered episodes of childhood, the city bum turned country tramp, suspicious, resentful, contemptuous of hick dumbness, bringing his own brand of violence into a world where he half-expected to find another kind, enough unlike his own to make him look over his shoulder down the empty lane as dusk came on, a creature altogether lost and pitiful, a dim image of what, in one perspective, our human condition is. But then, at that moment, I was merely thinking of the impingement of his loose-footedness and lostness on a stable and love-defined world of childhood.

Before the tramp actually appeared, I had, however, known he was coming, and without planning I began to write the fourth paragraph of the story, about the difference between what time is when we have grown up and what it was when we stood on what, in my fancy phrase in the story, I called the glistening auroral beach of the world—a phrase which belonged, by the way, to an inland boy who had never seen a beach but whose dreams were all of the sea. Now the tramp came up, not merely out of the woods, but out of the darkening grown-up world of time.

The tramp had, literally, come up through the river woods, and so in the boy's literal speculations he sees the tramp coming through the woods. By now, however, the natural thematic distinction touched on in relation to time is moving into a pattern, the repetition in fiction of the established notion in a new guise. So when the boy sees the mental image of the tramp coming through the woods, there is the distinction set up between the way a man, particularly such a man as this, would go through woods, and the way a boy can stand in the woods in absolute quiet, almost taking root and growing moss on himself, trying to catch the rhythm, as it were, of that vegetative life, trying to breathe himself into that mode of being.

But what would this other, woodland, vegetative world of being carry with it in human terms—in terms, that is, of what a story must be about? I can promise that the passage was written on impulse, but an impulse conditioned by the idea that there had to be an expressed difference between boy-in-woods and tramp-in-woods, the tramp who doesn't know what a poult is and thinks the final degradation is to mess with a flower bed. And so here we are back to the contrast between the tramp's world and that of childhood innocence appearing in some sense of a rapport between the child and nature, his feeling that he himself might enter that very life of nature.

As soon as the passage was written I knew its import; I was following my nose, trusting, for what they were worth, my powers of association, hoping that those powers would work in relation to a pattern that had begun to emerge as a series of contrasts. And it was natural, therefore, after a few paragraphs about the strangeness and fish-out-of-waterness of the tramp, his not knowing about dogs for example, to have the mother's self-sufficiency set against the tramp's rude, resentful uncertainty, and then have her portrait at the time of the episode set against the time when she would be dead, and only a memory—though back then, of course, in the secure world of changelessness and timelessness, it had never crossed the boy's mind that "she would ever be dead."

The instant I wrote that clause I knew, not how the story would end, for I was still writing by guess and by God, but on what perspective of feeling it would end. I knew that it would end with a kind of detached summary of the work of time, some hint of the adult's grim orientation toward that fact. From now on, the items that came on the natural wash of recollection came not only with their, to me, nostalgic quality, but also with the freighting of the grimmer possibilities of change—the flood, which to the boy is only an exciting spectacle but which will mean hunger to others, the boy's unconscious contempt for poor white-trash like Milt Alley, the recollection of hunger by the old man who had ridden with Forrest, Dellie suffering in her "woman mizry."

Part 2

But before I had got to Dellie, I already had Old Jebb firmly in mind, with some faint sense of the irony of having his name remind one—or at least me—of the dashing Confederate cavalryman killed at Yellow Tavern.

Perhaps what I finally did with Dellie stemmed, in fact, from the name I gave Old Jebb. Even if the boy would see no irony in that echo of J.E.B. Stuart's fame, he would get a shock when Dellie slapped her beloved son, and would sense that that blow was, in some deep way, a blow at him. I knew this, for I knew the inside of that prideful cabin, and the shock of early recognition that beneath mutual kindliness and regard some dark, tragic, unresolved something lurked. And with that scene with Dellie, I felt I was forecasting the role of the tramp in the story. The story, to put it in another way, was now shifting emphasis from the lyricism of nostalgia to a concern with the jags and injustices of human relationships. What had earlier come in unconsciously, reportorially, in regard to Milt Alley now got a conscious formulation.

I have said that the end was by now envisaged as a kind of summary of the work of time on the human relationships. But it could not afford to be a mere summary: I wanted some feeling for the boy's family and Jebb's family to shine through the flat surface. Now it struck me that I might build this summary with Jebb as a kind of pilot for the feeling I wanted to get; that is, by accepting, in implication at least, something of Jebb's feeling about his own life, we might become aware of our human communion. I wanted the story to give some notion that out of change and loss a human recognition may be redeemed, more precious for being no longer innocent. So I wrote the summary.

When I had finished the next to the last paragraph I still did not know what to do with my tramp. He had already snarled at the boy, and gone, but I sensed that in the pattern of things his meaning would have to coalesce with the meaning I hoped to convey in the summary about the characters. Then, for better or worse, there it was. In his last anger and frustration, the tramp had said to the boy: "You don't stop following me and I cut yore throat, you little son-of-a-bitch."

Had the boy then stopped or not? Yes, of course, literally, in the muddy lane. But at another level—no. Insofar as later he had grown up, had really learned something of the meaning of life, he had been bound to follow the tramp all his life, in the imaginative recognition, with all the responsibility which such a recognition entails, of this lost, mean, defeated, cowardly, worthless, bitter being as somehow a man.

So what had started out for me as, perhaps, an act of escape, of fleeing back into the simplicities of childhood, had turned, as it always must if we accept the logic of our lives, into an attempt to bring something meaningfully out of that simple past into the complication of the present. And what had started out as a personal indulgence had tried to be, in the end, an impersonal generalization about experience, as a story must always try to be if it accepts the logic of fiction. And now, much later, I see that the story and the novel which I had then only lately finished, as well as the study of Coleridge, all bore on the same end.

I would give a false and foolish impression if I were to imply that I think this to be the only way a story should be written, or that this is the only way I myself have ever written stories. As a matter of fact, most of my stories and all of my novels (except two unpublished ones) have started very differently, from some objective situation or episode, observed or read about, something that caught my eye and imagination so that feeling and interpretation began to flow in. And I sometimes think it strange that the last story I ever wrote and presumably the last I shall ever write (for poems are great devourers of stories) should have sprung so instinctively from the world of simple recollection—not a blackberry winter at all, but a kind of Indian summer.

I would give a false impression, too, if I were to imply that this story is autobiographical. It is not. I never knew these particular people, only that world and people like them. And no tramp ever leaned down at me and said for me to stop following him or he would cut my throat. But if one had, I hope that I might have been able to follow him anyway, in the way the boy in the story does.

On "The Patented Gate
and the Mean Hamburger"

The first sentence of the story reads: "You have seen him a thousand times." And I suppose I had seen him a thousand times, or men just like him, years before, when I was a boy. But his name was not Jeff York, the name of the man in the story as it now exists. As a matter of fact, I do not even remember what his name really was—though, even now, I see him clearly in my mind's eye, standing on the corner of a street in a little town, not belonging there on cement or brick, withdrawn into the fierce dignity of his kind and into his own obsessive dream. As for his name, it is improbable that, after all this time, anybody in the world remembers it—unless one of the towheads really existed and is alive and remembers the name of the man who happened to be his father and who put the .12 gauge to his head (or was it to his heart?) and pushed the trigger with a stick (or was it with his big toe, with the sock pulled off to make things easier?) and so settled his account with his dream. Head or heart, stick or big toe—the details of the real event were not important, and are long since lost.

The event itself was not important. A poor farmer, middle-aged and feckless, had sold his farm and moved to town, and didn't make out somehow, and so shot himself. Nobody knew him very well, he was a stand-offish sort of man, and once the body was below ground, wherever they put it below ground, the forgetting came easy.

The forgetting should have come even easier for me, for I had moved away long before, and had scarcely known the man, merely a figure seen now and then on the street or in some store, tall, bony, withdrawn, tough and dry as whit-leather. I would have forgotten him completely except for one thing. When, some weeks after the suicide, I happened to be back for a few days, somebody told me how Mr. ——

96

had got the habit of sitting around a store or garage brooding about the fact that he didn't have any land anymore. And somebody else happened to remark that he hadn't made such a hell of a living off the place anyhow, and it was sure lonesome out there for his wife, and she had made him move to town. I didn't know his wife, even by sight. I didn't know why he had come to town, perhaps to try to get a job even in that time (it was still the Depression) when jobs were hard to come by. But in any case, once he had lost that piece of land which he had sweated so long to get, he couldn't stand it. That piece of land was his identity. Landless, he was nothing.

So much for the facts of the case. It seemed like a story, and so I wrote a story. It turned out to be a very bad story. Nobody wanted to publish it, and after a few tries, I didn't want to publish it either. Anyway, by that time I was deep into a novel—which became my first published novel—and the story seemed trivial. I threw the manuscript aside and, for all practical purposes, forgot it.

Some eight or nine years, three novels, and a world war later, I remembered the story. At that time I was living, and had been living for a long time, about as far away from the world of Jeff York as one can get—in Minneapolis, in a tiny apartment over the garage of a mansion, a hulking and ugly relic of the lumber boom of some forty years before, and it was winter with the iron, bludgeoning cold of a Minnesota winter, and snow was heaped six feet deep at the sides of the alley leading to the garage. As for my inner world, I had lately finished a novel which had engaged me for a long time. I had had a long tussle with it, had done the best I could, and now I felt blank and used up. I suppose I was, in that period, looking backward, trying to locate myself, to get a fresh start. I was reading Herman Melville's poetry, the poems about the Civil War, and some books on American history, things that in themselves were backward-looking. It was one of the historical studies that somehow touched the secret switch of association. That book, in discussing the early migration from Virginia, Maryland, and Carolina, over the mountains, said that those pioneers who happened to come from hill country, where the soil was already washing away and the game shot out, would pass by rich bottom land to seek a region that reminded them of the home they had left—and their choice would, in the end, with erosion and commercial competition, confirm their doom of poverty. As I read that section I suddenly saw the face of the man whose name I could not remember but whose story now seemed, for the first time, truly real to me.

I then saw that the earlier version of the story had been thin and mechanical—a mere anecdote with a shocking end. What now seemed important was the sense of history encompassing and flowing into the man's life, and the sense of his struggle against the inherited doom which he did not understand. Then I thought of the situation which World War II had just made a commonplace of American life, the hordes of people, white and Negro, from the backcountry, from all the marginal farms and sharecropper's shacks and mountain coves, who flooded into Detroit and Akron and Chicago and the other great industrial cities of the North, where their inherited values and attitudes would not be relevant and where, though they might make a living, they might lose some sense of life-direction. I do not mean for one moment to imply that such migrants had left a rural Eden. There was no rural Eden. Most were landless in any case, or men whose land was ruined or inadequate to sustain them. But they had moved into what was for many of them, if we are to believe our own eyes and the testimony of sociologists and historians, a kind of limbo. Their deepest values had been called into question.

All this sounds very general and abstract, and we know that the general and abstract seem the very opposite of fiction, which deals with the particular, the concrete, the individual. How could these things make me feel, suddenly, that the life and death of the nameless man were important? No, "important" is not the right word. It was merely that as I saw that man in the perspective of history and in the perspective of a great social shift in our own time, I felt a surge of emotion. I do not mean to say that I felt this because I saw this man as "representative" of a class. On the contrary, I felt for the first time that I had some real appreciation of his personal toughness and valor. That is, I saw how great had been the odds against him. I saw how he had struggled to escape the doom of his luckless class and kind, and after success, had been caught in another doom, one that he did not know how to struggle against: he could not deny the wife, and yet if he surrendered to her desire, he could not bear the loss of the identity he had struggled so long to achieve.

So I began to write the story. I did not rewrite the old version. I did not even try to find the manuscript, at least I have no recollection of having done so. I wanted now to write directly out of the new feeling, and the new feeling had to do with trying to capture the sense of the place, which was so far away from the snow-jammed alley in Minneapolis, and to give a sense of the man standing alone against the backdrop, as it were, of history and the changing immediate world around him. In other words, for me, the force of the story of Jeff York was to be dependent, essentially, on the way it was "framed."

There are, of course, other people than Jeff in the story, and the people in a story should always have functions, have roles, and not be mere convenient pegs to hang action on. So Slick Hardin, who has had a touch of the outside world, even if he had failed there, cannot stay here. He feels superior to the old world. He wants to go back to Nashville to run a poolroom, the place where his dreary, supercilous jokes would be understood. The banker, too, is in the picture; he thinks that for a man to move to town is "to better himself." Furthermore, as a side element, an incidental irony which I hoped would accent the story, the banker is buying the land which is, literally, life and death to Jeff York, as a sort of toy for himself, to keep his Tennessee Walkers on.

There is, of course, the wife, and she is crucial. She had to be younger than Jeff. She had to be the only woman he had ever known. The situation, in other words, had to be such that he would be peculiarly vulnerable, would feel that if he lost her, there would never be another woman for him. At the same time that Jeff is peculiarly vulnerable to her, he had, without realizing it, somehow sacrificed her to his obsession. At least, she would have felt it that way. She is young; she yearns for some excitement. She yearns for the taste of beef after all the pork. She treasures the high-heeled shoes she scarcely knows how to walk in. Nothing is really her fault. She simply doesn't understand the nature of Jeff's dream, any more than he does.

Let us turn for a moment to the title of the story. I stuck it in on impulse, after the story was written. The gate is back in the story. It had not appeared in the first version, as well as I can now remember, but the shot-gun would be too easy and predictable, no novelty to it, and so the gate, the mark of Jeff's success, becomes, with a little twist of irony, the machine for his death. The hamburger, too, is in the story. Slick Hardin, in a moment of expansiveness, the money for the sale now being in his pocket, says condescendingly to Mrs. York: "Lady, . . . you sure fling a mean hamburger."

The two items, gate and hamburger, pop into my head. But now we may ask what logic may have lain behind that fact. The gate is "patented"—clever, efficient, belonging, if you will, to the world of the modern, to the town, or rather, to the prosperous farms beginning to be oriented toward town. The hamburger is "mean," a piece of Slick

Hardin's fatuous, would-be-funny, town lingo; but "mean" is a loaded word, with a double sense—*mean* in the slangy, town sense of tricky and expert, and *mean* as cruel, ferocious, destructive. So the elements merge in the title, as it popped into my head. It had popped in because it was in the story with, I hope, more than a mere factual relevance.

Not the title, nor anything else about the story, was planned out like a chess game. The hope is, when you write, that if you strike on the right feeling and the right line, things will develop along the way. You may throw out ten things before the thing pops into your head that has truly developed from the feeling and the idea. You have to be very critical of what pops into your head, but you have to be open, too, to whatever logic may lie behind the random notion. I remember, for instance, how the notion of the Tennessee Walkers, for better or for worse, got into the story—merely on impulse, as I worked on the dialogue with the banker. Slick Hardin's leaving for Nashville—that, too, was on impulse: all at once I saw the packed valise behind the counter. I did stop along the way to give some thought to the relationship between Jeff and his wife. The thought, however, was simply a way of trying to find the inside logic of the situation. And often such a logic develops, as I hope it does here, from the original germ of feeling which starts a story on its way.

Part 3

THE CRITICS

Introduction

As I indicated above, Robert Penn Warren's short fiction has not received the positive and careful attention accorded his poetry and longer fiction. Causes for this anomalous situation probably include Warren's relatively small body of short fiction, his own somewhat contradictory remarks on the genre, and the greater public and critical awareness of his poems, novels, and nonfiction works. Moreover, considerable division of interpretation and evaluation exist even in the relatively small number of studies of Warren's short fiction. Opinions on both sides are cited and analyzed in Part 1, and two representative, extended, and insightful examples are presented here. Allen G. Shepherd's article, published in 1979, represents the more negative view of the short fiction within the Warren canon, while Randolph Runyon's essay, published in 1985, proves more positive. Both pieces first appeared in *Mississippi Quarterly*, but Shepherd has published other work on the short fiction, while Runyon has revised and expanded his analysis as a chapter in his recent book on Warren's fiction (see Bibliography).

Allen G. Shepherd

Of the numerous genres in which Robert Penn Warren has worked over six decades, it is his achievement in short fiction which both the author himself and a good many of his readers have found least satisfying. Most of the stories are in fact surprisingly undistinguished, often either slight or awkwardly constructed. Explanations for his indifferent success in short fiction might start with the fact that Warren, when he wrote many of the stories collected in *The Circus in the Attic and Other Stories* (1948), was a beginner, at least in fiction. It is also the case, as Warren has conceded, that he wrote them for fast sale ("the quick buck. Which didn't come").[1] The stories did not, for the most part, represent major efforts; they were—to apply Arthur Miller's description of his own short stories—"what came easier."[2] Finally, and most importantly, the form itself seems to have inhibited Warren's natural talents and inclinations.

In writing short stories in the 1930's and '40's, Warren appears to have backed into an unhappy compromise; stories were neither long enough nor short enough, offered neither the satisfying extensive scope of the novel nor the demanding intensive concision of the poem. Warren the story teller shows to perhaps equally good advantage in "The Ballad of Billie Potts" and *Night Rider*; in contemporary short stories, by contrast, with a few notable exceptions, Warren the poet-novelist seems ill at ease, struggling to escape.[3]

The stories in *The Circus in the Attic*, Warren says, "were always a kind of accident," and there are few of them which he now likes at all.[4] "Short stories are out for me."[5] Only a handful of his collected stories merit individual consideration, and those three or four which do have been amply studied. But there have been few sustained attempts either to establish the place of the short stories in the canon or to discuss their interpretive use *vis-à-vis* Warren's poetry and novels.

Reprinted from "Prototype, Byblow and Reconception: Notes on the Relation of Warren's *The Circus In The Attic* to His Novels and Poetry," in *Mississippi Quarterly* 33 (Winter 1979–1980: 3–17. Reprinted with permission of the journal.

Thus the value of this and any further studies depends largely on the light they cast upon the relation of Warren's stories to his novels and poems.

Before turning briefly to Warren's own illuminating reflections on this relation, it seems appropriate to note that besides the twelve stories and two novellas in *The Circus in the Attic*, there were—at last count—fifteen uncollected stories, all of them pre-publication excerpts from his novels.[6] Of these, "Cass Mastern's Wedding Ring," 1944 (*All the King's Men*) remains both best and best known; the most recent extract is "Life and Death with Agnes," 1977 (*A Place to Come To*).[7] The generally high quality of these stories, which usually figure in the novels as vignettes, *exempla*, or secondary plots, suggests that Warren often composes his best short stories as a practicing novelist. Such embedded stories, that is, benefit greatly in their coherence and conclusiveness from the layered density of context which a novel-length narrative provides.[8]

In his farewell to the short story, first printed in 1959[9] but whose content he has subsequently reiterated and expanded upon for a succession of interviewers, Warren spoke of his discovery that "the overlap between the short story and the poem was very bad for me," principal evidence of which was his inability to finish a single short poem for almost a decade, beginning about 1944. During those ten years Warren reassessed what he came to feel was his overly abstract view of the germ of a poem, and when in the mid-1950's he went back to short poems, he found that they "were more directly tied to a realistic base of facts, . . . more tied up with an event, an anecdote, an observation . . . were tied more directly to the sort of thing that might become a short story. . . . So most of the short poems," he concluded, "that is, many, many, many since then, could easily have turned into a short story."[10] I expect that any reader of Warren's later poetry could compile a list of poems which might in other times have become stories, though probably few would regret that this did not occur.

Examination of the connection between story and poem, then, as between story and novel, must extend beyond a recitation of parallels, since those connections are frequently intimate, sometimes complex, occasionally crucial to an understanding of both. Inevitably one must indulge in some speculation as to the stages in the evolution of thematic and other concerns recurring in two or more genres. When, as will be indicated, decades pass between Warren's engagement and subsequent re-engagement with such concerns, it stands to reason, though it is difficult to prove, that that re-engagement has been affected by other intervening work. The problem is not of tracing revisions; the problem is of balancing our recognition of sometimes striking parallels against our awareness of Warren's customary artistic practice—of reconceiving, that is, imagining anew, essential issues.

To develop these problems further and to arrive at some tentative solutions, four stories are to be examined: "Prime Leaf," "The Circus in the Attic," "When the Light Gets Green," and "Goodwood Comes Back." In their relation to poems and novels they will figure as prototype, byblow, and reconception, categories which are of necessity not mutually exclusive. Because it can be stated most succinctly and demonstrated most clearly, a story as prototype of a novel will serve as our first illustration.

Several of the collected stories seem unmistakably to be sketches toward or prototypes of either a novel or a poem or poems. One such instance, noted in passing by a contemporary reviewer of *The Circus in the Attic*[11] and subsequently developed and made familiar by a number of essayists, is the prototypical relation between Warren's first published novella, "Prime Leaf" (1930), and his first published novel, *Night Rider* (1939), which I think requires little recapitulation here.[12] The relation is both extensive and unique, and in the novella one witnesses Warren exploring and developing the history, locale, traditions, values, characters and themes to which he would return in the novel.

More important to the present purpose than the further citation of familiar evidence is the indication which this connection provides: from the beginning of his career as a novelist Warren was in the habit of reinvestigating characters, situations, and themes earlier set down in short fiction, of recasting in more answerable form the essence of fiction—the image of meaning emerging from experience. Comparative study of story and novel or story and poem may help to accomplish what James Justus has rightly said needs doing: "to see *how* the themes emerge from the textual density of the created worlds . . . ,"[13] particularly in worlds so intimately related.

The last written of the novellas, "The Circus in the Attic" (1947), which Warren admits he still likes "very much, relatively speaking,"[14] offers a case in point more complicated than the first written.[15] The collection's title story reinforces the general impression that Warren is not a natural short-story writer, as was Faulkner or Hemingway, and that over seventeen years he had not really mastered the form. Indeed, one might argue that—considered on its own terms and despite certain amateurish touches—"Prime Leaf" is the better, assuredly the more coherent and controlled work. The proto-novelistic qualities of characterization, plot, structure and theme in "The Circus in the Attic" further suggest that for Warren the overlap of novella and novel could be only somewhat less dangerous than that of short story and poem.

Such recognition gives added point to Warren's praise of Katherine Anne Porter, who has, he says, "a genius for short fiction. The amount of density, of philosophical density, the human weight that she can get into things like 'Old Mortality'! It's as big as a big novel."[16] Exactly such philosophical density, human weight, resonance was what Warren was after in this ambitious, badly flawed novella. That he failed, that "The Circus in the Attic" is, as Charles Bohner has rightly observed, "rambling and diffuse," "more a synopsis of a Warren novel than a fully realized short story,"[17] may serve both to rationalize Warren's feeling that "short stories always seemed to have a way of limiting your risk in fiction"[18] and to focus upon the problematical relation the novella bears to *All the King's Men*.

The relation is not as close or as nearly programmatic as that of "Prime Leaf" to *Night Rider*, since "The Circus in the Attic" is not a prototype but a kind of byblow of the prolonged creative effort which produced *All the King's Men* in its evolving forms, beginning with a five-act verse play, *Proud Flesh*, of 1937, and continuing forty-one years later with the opera *All the King's Men* commissioned for production by the Kennedy Center for the Performing Arts.

"The Circus in the Attic" was written in 1946 and published in September 1947. Major rewriting of *All the King's Men* continued into March 1946, and the novel was published in August of that year. This is to say that Warren was working on both novella and novel in the same year. Composition of "The Circus in the Attic" followed, chronologically, several versions of the verse play referred to, a number of poems thematically related to the novel, and the short story "Cass Mastern's Wedding Ring." Of the works written before the novella, however, none seems so closely related to it in characterization, theme, and style, if not consistently in plot, as does the novel.

Though most if not all of Warren's fiction suffers by comparison with his premier novel, comparison of novella and novel is validated by such connections of characterization, plot and theme as the following: both protagonists are only children of aristocratic lineage; both possess weak fathers and dominant mothers, and both drift by default out of potentially redemptive love affairs. Both are students of the past and reporters of the present, for whom the accumulation of facts is easy, their interpretation difficult. Both retreat from the world into life-defying closed systems, and both arc in search of a hero, whose violent death produces climax and resolution.

We enter what may well seem familiar territory in the novella on a "sun-glazed highway [which] spins off ahead of you, down the valley, like a ribbon of celluloid film carelessly unspooled across green baize."[19] We don't encounter either the hypnotic rhythm or the compressed-spring tension of the opening passages of *All the King's Men* down Highway 58, but we are at once put in the company of an anonymous narrator, who in his occasionally sardonic, tough-talking irony recalls Jack Burden and who shares Burden's awareness of glittering modernity laid over old country. Unfortunately for the novella, our nameless guide shortly loses both independent identity and consistent touch with the telling, and we are left to heavily freighted authorial commentary, which does not, however, disguise the story's lack of narrative control. A Burden-like narrator or narrator-protagonist seems, in fact, precisely what the novella needs.

Bolton Lovehart, the frail, frustrated, aristocratic protagonist of this drama, may be construed as a Jack Burden who never ventures into the great world of people and power and who is a trapped victim. The site of his labors is the Haunted Palace of History, in which he pathetically fails to achieve the deepest desires of all Warren's protagonists—to be free and himself.

Born an only child into a privileged home to a weak father, who dies while Bolton is still young, and a dominant mother of near-cannibalistic possessiveness, he makes several abortive escape attempts; he is for his indecisiveness seduced and abandoned by a local girl, before finally acceding to his public role as semi-professional local historian. Later in life he finds a hero in his braggart stepson, a posthumous Medal of Honor winner, and becomes for a time in his reflected energy and glory a current-affairs expert, reporter of sorts. All this precedes his climactic return to the creation of those small, inanimate, innocent objects whose world alone he cherishes, controls, and understand.

"The Circus in the Attic" is essentially a story about history, the meaning and interpretation of the living past as it impinges on the present, the study of history being what Warren calls "man's long effort to be human."[20] The loss of that past is virtually equivalent to a loss of existence itself, and indeed Lovehart's is less a fully human life than a biological simulacrum. He "survives as the central figure," Leonard Casper notes, "only by force of accident." It may also be true, as Casper suggests, that "the storytelling method . . . seems to assent to, rather than censure, the notion that all men are equally unimportant—that each simply has his own source of intoxication, his own dark compulsion and destiny, his own mystification."[21] Yet Warren's aim in the novella, as I understand it, was to work through a series of hypotheses, each associated with characters whose lives are epitomized for us in a series of often fine vignettes. He sought, further, to dramatize the elements of the problem of the apprehension of historical causation and truth, carrying reader and surviving characters, Lovehart included, to a resolution necessarily provisional but validated by the range of human evidence presented.

The chorus of characters' truths, however, offers no sort of thematic harmony, familiar as a number of authorial pronouncements may sound. Thus, in good philosophical Burdenesque style: "Man wants to know the truth and if he knows the truth . . . ," which is observed with respect to Major Simon Lovehart, C. S. A., Bolton's father, "who carries with him the explanation of everything" (p. 18). So do most of the other characters, which accounts in essence for the failure of the novella; it does not reach a conclusion, it ends. Warren does not impose a meaning on the characters' experience, a fault with which he is sometimes justifiably charged. We are left instead with a sad little foetus of truth which has not had either proper conditions or sufficient time to develop.

The senior Lovehart carries a minnie ball in his thigh and it is his truth, explains everything. Jack Burden, historical researcher and philosophical thinker, might well have understood and integrated this "one-answer" man into his narrative and scheme; by contrast, in "The Circus in the Attic," Major Lovehart's hypothesis is set up, briefly developed, but then left hanging, unapprehended by his son, as one of a series of dissociated vignettes. Warren is fully capable of weaving together numerous story-size narratives, as his virtuoso performance in *The Cave* demonstrates. But in the novella he seems to have invented characters he doesn't see as people and whom he doesn't know as a writer. What is wrong with the Major Lovehart sequence, as with the whole novella, is that it lacks a sufficiently coherent context and an adequately perceptive interpreter. In a novel Warren could have carried it off, but not in shorter fiction.

The novella is caught in the overlap of whose dangers Warren spoke, and it suffers accordingly. In "The Circus in the Attic," Warren's structural-thematic technique is much like that in his novels: alternatives, opposites, and contraries are examined, arranged, and rearranged like pieces in a jigsaw puzzle. But whereas in *All the King's Men*, and to a lesser extent in *World Enough and Time*, an illuminated design emerges, in the novella the resulting image is so dark and discontinuous as to be almost incomprehensible.

At the conclusion of the novella, in the summary of all the principal characters' fates and of Janie Murphy Parton James's future prospects, Warren appears to make one final effort to cast a retrospective thematic coherence over his story. To this end he draws on Jack Burden's theories of historical costs and the moral neutrality of history. The former affirms the evil and suffering involved in history, while the latter posits the idea that history itself has no inherent values, that meaning comes from man. Janie James, widow of Bolton's stepson, is one of very few characters in the novella who seems—through love, anguish, guilt, joy, and a sense of sin—to have achieved the beginning of virtue, to have learned something which will profit her.

Though she does not dramatically walk out into the awful responsibility of Time, she is aware—as Burden was—of the contrast between the brute forces of history and the limited but real efficacy of human values and appears to have accepted the human responsibility of learning values from history. We wish her well, but on all other fronts history has won and the glory of her human effort seems vestigial; it is too little and too late.

What then, finally, may be said of the relation of "The Circus in the Attic" to *All the King's Men*? In characterization, theme, style, and even, initially, in point of view, resemblances between novella and novel may be detected, yet they cannot legitimize "The Circus in the Attic." Byblow seems aptly descriptive as summary: a side, or indirect, blow; hence, also, an incidental mischance; thus, a bastard.

Contemporaneity of composition is only one of the features which distinguishes the relation between "The Circus in the Attic" and *All the King's Men* from the relation to one of Warren's most successful stories, "When the Light Gets Green" (1936), to two poems, "Court-Martial" (1957) and "A Confederate Veteran Tries to Explain the Event" (1966). Consider first the story and the earlier poem. In the story, old Mr. Barden, the narrator's grandfather, shortly emerges from the fairy-tale image ("My grandfather had a long white beard and sat under the cedar tree" [p. 88]) which introduces him and the story. He becomes one of the heroic combatants, as Arthur Mizener has said, in "the necessarily uncomprehending and hopeless fight that love and pride put up against change and time."[22] The other combatant, his grandson, suffers the guilt of having tried and failed both to feel and to speak the impossible love the old man needed. Warren takes full advantage of the dramatic possibilities inherent in the story's point of view, staying within the limits of the boy's understanding, directing our attention to seemingly irrelevant contingencies, while setting down the sad account of what happened.

Twenty-one years later, in "Court-Martial," Warren returned to grandfather, Captain, Cavalry, C. S. A., and grandson under the same cedar tree; the boy now seeks "somehow, to untie / The knot of History," past registered as clearly distinct from future; "And the *done* and the *to-be-done* / In that timelessness were one, / Beyond the poor *being done*." But the old man this time destroys that false hope by climactically launching into a violent and grisly account of what he and his men had long ago in the war done with bushwhackers. " 'By God—' and he jerked up his head. / 'By God, they deserved it,' he said. / Don't look at me that way,' he said." What the boy, his childhood over, now sees and judges is his grandfather "Not old now, not old now, but young," pursued by a visionary company of his late victims, "Each face outraged, agape"; he sees the world as *being done*, the past as actual, and he suddenly knows "The world is real. It is there."[23] Story and poem derive from the same substance, but draw from it notably different meanings.

Nine years later, in "A Confederate Veteran Tries to Explain the Event" (1966), Warren circled back to "the old man sitting under the cedar" and his grandson, certain at age nine that "there must be a *why*," a true and preferably simple explanation for a neighbor's shocking suicide. And there is an answer, though the truth which the old man articulates is unexpected and unsettling: " 'For some folks the world gets too much!' "[24] If one can conceive of a generic grandfather, sitting under a generic cedar tree, and equally at home in the story and two poems, then perhaps one can also conceive of the generic grandson grappling with questions whose answers will illuminate both his own and the great world. This is to say that Warren does not simply sharpen old meanings but discovers new ones.

This trio, written over thirty years, is unusual in at least two respects. First, the early story stands comparison with two good later

111

poems. Second, although a single rather abstract statement of theme comprehends all three (the truth of the real world discoverable only there, action and thought and accident commingled), story and poems are less variations on a theme than puzzling truth three times fronted, twice reconceived.

It will not do to call the story a prototype of the poems, and application of the term *byblow* to either story or poems is even less appropriate. To speak of the three as constituting variations on a theme is closer to the truth but also fails to capture the essence of the artistic-philosophical process apparent in the sequence. As Warren's observations in several of the interviews previously cited make clear, story and poems recall his childhood. Instead of refashioning recollection in three complementary ways, Warren has built the first poem on the story, the second poem on both the story and the first poem. The process is cumulative; much is added, but nothing essential is lost. Stories, Warren has said, destroy poems. "When the Light Gets Green" seems to posit a corollary: not if one is patient.

As one of the most successful stories in *The Circus in the Attic*, "When the Light Gets Green" may well be termed atypical. For the sake, then, of representative selection, and, more importantly, because it illustrates a different kind of relation between a story and a poem, we may next consider "Goodwood Comes Back" (1941).

Among the failings common to the slighter stories in *The Circus in the Attic* are Warren's use of an imperceptive or inscrutable narrator, awkward plotting, shallow irony, and a gratuitous, mechanically violent ending, all of which are apparent in varying degree in "Goodwood Comes Back." Luke Goodwood, friend of the narrator's youth, rises to brief Big League stardom as a World Series pitcher with the Athletics, succumbs to alcohol, and comes home to hunt and farm, principally the former. Before long he is murdered by his brother-in-law, killed with his own shotgun, a catcher at last.

All of this is recorded in a curiously ambivalent tone, which makes it appear that the narrator either does not know or does not wish to know what he feels about Goodwood's life and death. The fact that the narrator, who has also moved away, received intelligence of Goodwood's rise and fall in a series of a half-dozen letters from his hometown sister further reinforces a sense of his maintaining a perhaps self-preserving distance from the tale he tells. By far the most effective part of the story focuses on their last meeting, during which one comes to understand—as well as the story's limitations permit—the two men and the nature of their relationship.

Thirty-five years after the story was published, Warren returned to the characters, the scene, and many of the events, as if to set right in verse what had failed in prose. The poem is "American Portrait: Old Style" (1976),[25] and it demonstrates once again both Warren's established habit of re-engaging the material of his short stories and his ability to reinterpret and to make their substance new.

In *Now and Then*, the poem introduces Part I, "Nostalgic"; appropriately enough, "American Portrait: Old Style" is about going home. The portrait is of two men, each of them as he was and as he is. What both will come to is intimated by the paired images which open and close the poem, "the nameless old skull" and "the trench, six feet long" (pp. 3, 7). Mutability, then, and one's resources for contending with mortality constitute the poem's ground theme. From the story it is possible to infer such concerns, but in "American Portrait" Warren achieves an intensification of focus, a surety of structure and hence a clarity of statement which are wholly alien to "Goodwood Comes Back." It is within the context of such essential distinctions that the parent similarities between story and poem should be weighed.

The narrator of the poem and his boyhood friend, here called K but in virtually all respects Goodwood's double, grow up and apart, K to brief success in the Big Leagues, where "no batter / Could do what the booze finally did: / Just blow him off the mound" (p. 5). K comes back, to farm a little and to hunt with his dogs.

Similarities of action and phrasing, perhaps most striking, merit at least one illustration. Thus Goodwood, to demonstrate to local moralists that even after coming back he still has an arm, scoops up a rock and fires it at a telephone pole, hits it, and yells, "Still got control, boys!" (p. 114). K, for an audience of one, "Snatched a stone, wound up, and let fly, / And high on a pole over yonder the big brown insulator / Simply exploded. 'See—I still got control!' he said" (p. 6).

In "Goodwood Comes Back" Warren's interest seems largely concentrated on introducing the characters, a number of whom prove to be inconsequential, and on deepening the realistic texture of the narrative with half-suppressed tonal ambivalence. In the poem the narrator finds positive assertion of life's final joyfulness difficult, painfully reminded as he is of its mysteries and tragedies, of K's life come to nothing, for example. Remembering "that last summer / [When] I was almost ready to learn / What imagination is— . . ." focusses upon his present faith:

113

". . . it is only / The lie we must live by, if ever / We mean to live at all" (p. 4).

The latter half of the poem brings the two men together after almost sixty years; they talk, though not easily, and Warren edges toward an epiphany. "Sun low, all silence, then sudden: / 'But Jesus,' he [K] cried, 'what makes a man do what he does— / Him living until he dies!'" Warren offers the reader his best answer, accepting both the painful necessity of the question and K's proud and pathetic assertion of retained "control," knowing the sky drifts on, "like forever, / From *where* on to *where*," and concludes with a response which honors both the inescapable truth of the real world and the necessity of man's hope: "And I love the world even in any anger, / And love is a hard thing to outgrow" (p. 8).

Goodwood did come back, after thirty-five years, in "American Portrait," the connection perhaps most pointedly attested to by nearly identical phrasing. By bringing him back, as "K," Warren marks but one advance in the poem over the story. In "American Portrait" Warren, firmly in control, holds to the proper limits of the germinal anecdote, gaining depth by concentration, and thus obviating problems of perception and tone. The somewhat mechanical violence of the story, e.g., the killing off of Goodwood, and its rather labored plotting, e.g., the epistolary exchanges between the narrator and his sister, never threaten the poem.

"American Portrait" will serve as a final example of Warren's powers of reconception—of re-imagining, refining, reshaping, and hence giving new life to the shadow poem he knows exists behind even such a narrative as "Goodwood Comes Back."

Throughout this essay I have assumed that Warren's best three or four stories, in which number I include "Blackberry Winter," "Christmas Gift," "The Patented Gate and the Mean Hamburger," and "When the Light Gets Green," are generally recognized for what they are: short fiction of a high order. The attempt to see one of these stories and others from *The Circus in the Attic* in relation to and as aids to the interpretation of Warren's poems and novels should not obscure the collection's intrinsic merit.

"Prime Leaf," whatever its deficiencies, marked a promising entry into fiction, and Warren remembers that its composition produced "a sense of freedom and excitement."[26] Long before his last novella, "The Circus in the Attic," however, that sense had become one of risks limited in an ancillary genre, of stories as accidental, or, worse, as dangerously overlapping with and potentially destructive of both novels and poems. Though Warren has continued to publish stories since 1948, some fine ones, they have all been pre-publication excerpts from his novels.

As examination of the metamorphoses of the collected stories has indicated, neither "When the Light Gets Green" nor "Goodwood Comes Back," though of widely different artistic merit, has proven sufficient end or adequate expression in itself. Study of the stories in the context of the canon strengthens our sense of the evolutionary nature of Warren's art through decades and genres and gives reason to expect that thirty years and more after the last story's composition, *The Circus in the Attic* will continue to fulfill its promise in other forms more congenial to the artist's powers.

Notes

1. Ruth Fisher, "A Conversation with Robert Penn Warren," *Four Quarters*, 21 (May 1972), 9. Hereafter cited as *Four Quarters*.

2. *Writers at Work: The Paris Review Interviews* (New York: Viking Press, 1967), p. 201.

3. Warren describes the connection between writing novels and writing poems as "some kind of cross-fertilization. And more and more since I quit writing stories. . . . The construction of a novel, though, and the construction of a poem are very close. Even behind a realistic narrative, there is—for me—a shadow poem" ("An Interview with Robert Penn Warren and Eleanor Clark," *New England Review*, 1 [Fall 1978], 66). Hereafter cited as *New England Review*.

4. *Four Quarters*, p. 9.

5. Richard Sale, "An Interview in New Haven with Robert Penn Warren," *Studies in the Novel*, 12 (Fall 1970), 340. Hereafter cited as *Studies in the Novel*.

6. This figure does not include unpublished stories.

7. "Life and Death with Agnes," *The Ohio Review*, 18 (Winter 1977), 49–74, is one of two pre-publication excerpts from *A Place to Come To*; the other is "Chicago," *The Georgia Review*, 30 (Winter 1976), 799–823.

8. Two of the weaker collected stories, "Testament of Flood" and "The Love of Elsie Barton," which derive from *God's Own Time* (1932–1933), a fragmentary, unpublished novel, are only apparent exceptions.

9. "Writer at Work: How a Story Was Born and How, Bit by Bit, It Grew," *New York Times Book Review*, March 1, 1959, pp. 4–5, 36.

10. *Studies in the Novel*, pp. 340–341. In a subsequent interview, Warren expanded on the relation of poem to story and novel. ". . . well, poetry is different from fiction. It's much more inside: you're reliving your life. For me, anyway. When I quit writing short stories I felt a great relief, because I had

been killing poems to write short stories. The small anecdote—the suggestion behind the anecdote—was a poem. And when you start telling a story, making the suggestion into a story, you start mucking the poem up. As the germ of a poem, it can grow" (*New England Review*, p. 65).

11. Robert Daniel, "No Place to Go," *Sewanee Review*, 55 (Summer 1948), 525.

12. Anyone interested in such recapitulation may consult the present writer's "Robert Penn Warren's 'Prime Leaf' as Prototype of *Night Rider*," *Studies in Short Fiction*, 7 (Summer 1970), 469–471. Warren speaks of the novella as the "germ" of the novel in *Writers at Work: The Paris Review Interviews*, ed. Malcolm Cowley (New York: Viking Press, 1959), p. 191. Hereafter cited as *Writers at Work*.

13. Review of Barnett Guttenberg's *Web of Being: The Novels of Robert Penn Warren*, *American Literature*, 48 (March 1976), 94.

14. *Four Quarters*, p. 9.

15. The prime depository of Warren's manuscripts is the Beinecke Library at Yale. Of the stories in *The Circus in the Attic*, only the title story exists there in significant variants. There is one typed copy marked "first draft," one marked "typescript," and one marked "deleted," which appears to be a carbon of the "typescript." The "first draft" is approximately 53⅛ pages long, while the "typescript," from which the printed story derives, is approximately 56¾ pages long. The three-page addition consists largely of supplemental detail and does not reflect any change in the author's conception.

16. *Studies in the Novel*, pp. 351–352.

17. *Robert Penn Warren* (New York: Twayne, 1964), p. 105.

18. *Four Quarters*, p. 9.

19. *The Circus in the Attic and Other Stories* (New York: Harcourt, Brace and World, n.d.), p. 3. Subsequent quotations will be identified in the text.

20. Transcript of "Conversation with Robert Penn Warren," "Bill Moyer's Journal," *PBS*, April 4, 1976, p. 2.

21. *Robert Penn Warren: The Dark and Bloody Ground* (Seattle: University of Washington Press, 1960), p. 99.

22. *A Handbook for Use with Modern Short Stories: The Uses of Imagination*, rev. ed. (New York: Norton, 1966), p. 151.

23. *Promises: Poems 1954–1956* (New York: Random House, 1957), pp. 22 and 23.

24. *Selected Poems: New and Old, 1923–1966* (New York: Random House, 1966), pp. 61 and 62.

25. The poem was published originally in *The New Yorker*, 52 (August 23, 1976), 26–27, and then collected—in revised form—in *Now and Then: Poems 1976–1978* (New York: Random House, 1978), pp 3–7. Citations will refer to *Now and Then*.

26. *Writers at Work*, p. 191.

Randolph Runyon

The Circus in the Attic has not fared well among Warren critics. Allen Shepherd finds most of the fourteen stories in the collection "surprisingly undistinguished, often either slight or awkwardly constructed."[1] Leonard Casper calls some of them "clumsy and predictable"[2] and others "contrived," although he admires the "authentic simplicity" of a few.[3] It is remarkable that James Justus, otherwise so comprehensive, does not even discuss the book as a whole, makes no mention of nine of its stories and has little to say about any of the others except "Prime Leaf," which interests him chiefly to the extent that it is an early version of *Night Rider*.[4] Charles Bohner speaks for most when he declares that the "prodigality of Warren's talent, his gift for sustained narrative and invention, seems cramped within the confines of the short story."[5]

Warren himself appears to concur in this negative view when he confesses that these stories "were always a kind of accident,"[6] and when he complains that when he wrote them he "had been killing poems to write short stories."[7] But an author is not always his best critic; sometimes the work itself, in ways no one has yet noticed, can provide the key to its own interpretation. Such is the case with *The Circus in the Attic*, which gives us its clue in the title story. The prophetic lines in question make reference in their immediate context to words that, like themselves, cannot be interpreted until the passage of time makes their context clear: "[N]o one knows the meaning of the cry of passion he utters until the flesh of the passion is long since withered away to show the austere, logical articulation of fact with fact in the skeleton of Time."[8] The father of Bolton Lovehart, protagonist of the first story of the collection, had just fallen victim to a stroke as he was walking up the brick path to his house. The cry of passion was uttered by Bolton's mother, "wild cries of anguish that might have

Reprinted from "The View from the Attic: Robert Penn Warren's *Circus* Stories," in *Mississippi Quarterly* 38 (Spring 1985): 119–35. Reprinted with the permission of the journal.

117

been wild cries of triumph"—which indeed they proved to be "in the sequel" (p. 28), this illustrating the truth of the subsequent declaration that the passage of time reveals the true meaning of a cry of passion. That such a revelation should come through a certain "articulation" is particularly revealing, for this well-chosen word's double meaning precisely articulates the separation between enunciation and connection, the divergence between passionate self-expression and cold, bony fact. One kind of articulation, in the passage of time, gives way to another.

What makes it possible to see in this narrator's remark a useful clue for reading the story, and with it the book of the same name, is the way it articulates (or articulates with) the central image of the narrative, the toy circus in the attic that Bolton Lovehart spends his life putting together. Lovehart's supposed writing of a local history serves as a cover for his real activity: When the paints for his wood-carved animals arrive he tells his mother they're for a multi-colored map of the county; when people pass by the house late at night and see his attic light burning they marvel at his authorial industry. The circus represents Bolton's escape from responsibility and the meshes of a possessive mother, and is a kind of substitute for the circus he tried to run away and join as a child. But there is another way of understanding his model menagerie: It *is* a kind of writing, even a way of writing the history of the county. When the narrator himself gives us a bit of that history we can see how close Bolton came to capturing the spirit of the place. On December 16, 1861, "Bardsville had its home guard, a few middle-aged men and a rag-tag-and-bobtail of young boys who could ride like circus performers and shoot anything that would hold powder and to whom the war was a gaudy picnic that their tyrannous mothers would not let them attend" (p. 6). Bolton could have done worse than debunk local mythology and portray the mock heroics of the town's defenders as the circus stunts they were. Thanks to the narrator's manipulation of events, to the way he allows us to see the resemblance between the home guards and the circus Bolton ran away to at sixteen and later duplicated at his leisure, Lovehart almost seems to be doing that, though it would never occur to us that he intended his toy circus to be taken as a revisionist reading of history. His circus was something more like a cry of passion, a way of bolting the attic door against a tyrannous mother; it is only in the connection, in the articulation of his circus pastime with the other facts of the story that the skeletal, structural logic of the narrative emerges. It was on the near-anniversary of the battle of Bardsville—"One day in middle December" (p. 10)—that Bolton passed by the local hardware store and saw the model circus that was to inspire his efforts. Bolton would not have grasped the irony of this fact, but we can, and we can see as well that in playing with his model men and animals he was rehearsing not only the circus antics that gave his father's generation the illusion of escape from a tyrannical maternity but also the ludic manipulation exercised by that same maternal tyranny. For Lovehart also bore a resemblance to his trapeze artists and ringmaster and cleverly constructed tigers with bendable, jointed (articulated) legs because of the way his mother is said to have created and governed him, possessing him "with a thousand invisible threads controlling the slightest movement of his limbs and lips and spirit like a clever puppet" (p. 16).

It is one thing to appreciate a story for what it seems to want to express—for its "authentic simplicity"[9] or psychological astuteness[10] or because through it the author "represents an aspect of the alienation wrought by the Southern caste system."[11] It is quite another to see it in light of what it actually does, to trace its articulations after the warmth of that willing authorial voice has died away. These stories already come to us at some remove from their first appearance, already some distance along on the time-line that leads from one kind of articulation to another, for all had appeared earlier, separately, in print.[12] Their collective appearance brings with it a whole new set of articulations, for the reader of the book can take into account something the reader of the stories in their first magazine appearances could not—the ways they connect with each other. An authorial note tells us that in one sense, at least, the book is a new creation and not merely the reprinting of what has appeared elsewhere: "The earliest story in this book was written in 1930, the latest in 1946, but the order here is not chronological" (unnumbered page between acknowledgments and page 1).[13] There are thus two new sources of the articulation of fact with fact: ways in which one story may cast new light on another (by the same kind of resemblance as that which a single story leads us to reinterpret, for example, Bolton's circus performers in light of the fact that some of the characters in the history he was supposed to be writing were described as circus performers by the narrator) and ways that the ordering itself of the stories (more precisely, the contiguity of certain stories) reinforces some of these resemblances—for on more than one occasion a similar event or image or turn of phrase will recur in two contiguous stories. A reader who approaches *The Circus in the Attic* as a single work of art and who attends to the subtle resonances set up by the way the stories echo fragments of each other might well begin to feel that there is yet another story being told here, one that can be at times discerned through the patient articulation of fact with fact, by piecing together the pattern of these recurring fragments. If he pursues that end, he will be following the lead given in the narrator's comment on the effect of time on the meaning of Mrs. Lovehart's cries, here equivalent to whatever purposes of plot and meaning each of the stories first served when published separately; the "flesh" of the first "passion" will wither away and reveal the hidden inner logic that unites the stories in this collection. What, in a reading of the stories as separate entities, might seem mere background material, now impresses the reader as an insistent repetition of certain actions, names, images and even homely household objects; the repeated details themselves assume a semblance of narrative meaning of their own.

Take, for example, an incident in "Blackberry Winter," the second story in the collection (and most beloved of critics), that take on a certain tinge of irony when we discover that we have already seen its ghostly inversion in the preceding story (if we read the stories in their sequence in the book). Seth, the boy protagonist of the story, has wandered out to gaze at the flooded creek. He sees his father on horseback among the crowd of onlookers.

> . . . the first thing that happened was, I remember, the warm feeling I always had when I saw him up on a horse. . . . I heard his voice calling, "Seth!" . . . I did not look up at my father until I was almost within touching distance of his heel. Then I looked up and tried to read his face, to see if he was angry about my being barefoot. Before I could decide anything from that impassive, high-boned face, he had leaned over and reached a hand to me. "Grab on," he commanded. (pp. 73–74)

Whatever misgivings the boy will have about the unseasonably cool weather or the tramp with the knife or the way Dellie slaps her son, his father will remain an undiminished source of confidence and love. He won't be angry, as Seth's mother was, about the bare feet. " 'You can see better up here,' " he will say when he swings the boy up to the saddle. But the reader who can recall a strangely similar event in "The Circus in the Attic," the immediately preceding story, will not so easily share this faith in a father's affection, for he will have remembered what happened to another Seth when he approached a man on a horse. Though a monument was erected to his memory, Seth Sykes did not exactly die a hero's death in the battle of Bardsville. He was simply objecting to the Union cavalry's expropriation of his corn.

> Seth Sykes came on and the troopers watched him. He grabbed the lieutenant's near leg, the left leg, and shouted, "Hit is my cawn!"
>
> The lieutenant leaned over and struck him about the head with his gauntleted fist. The horse shied and the lieutenant almost reeled from the saddle.
>
> But the nearest trooper was on them now. He leaned from his saddle, seized Seth Sykes by the long, uncombed, matted hair, jerked his head back, and carefully put the muzzle of a pistol against the head, just above the ear, and pulled the trigger. (p. 11)

It is the small details that are troubling. The father "had leaned over and reached a hand"; the lieutenant "leaned over and struck . . . with his . . . fist." Seth Sykes had grabbed the lieutenant's leg; the younger Seth gauges how close he had come to his father by the fact that he was "almost within touching distance of his heel." And then of course there is the fact of the name: Although we are at the midpoint of the story, it is only when the boy hears his father's voice calling "Seth!" that we learn his name; in fact, the name never reappears in "Blackberry Winter"—almost as if the boy were fully Seth only at the moment he and his father repeated those gestures of Seth Sykes's martyrdom.[14]

"The Circus in the Attic" contains other premonitions of what will happen in the stories that follow. Near the end of that first story, Bolton Lovehart's wife dies when the car she is riding in crashes "at high speed into the back of a heavy truck parked on the shoulder of the highway" (p. 60); "The Confession of Brother Grimes" will open with the account of how Grimes's daughter died in a nearly identical accident, when Archie Munn drove his car "through the back end of a parked truck" (p. 170). In a more elaborate interplay, the parasitical vines that afflict the cedar tree overshadowing the old Sykes house ("the single scrofulous cedar, weathering to earth and surrendering to the clawing hands of vine and briar" [p. 4] and cover the monument to Sykes and Perkins erected by the loving hands of the Daughters of the Confederacy ("If you tear away the love vine from the gray granite . . . you can read the words" [p. 5]) initiate an association of vines and other parasitical vegetation with femininity and of wood with manhood that will persist throughout the book. In "The Patented Gate and the Mean Hamburger" Jeff York's face is likened to "a piece of hewed cedar which has been left in the weather" (p. 120); his "long wrist bones hang out from the sleeves of the coat, the tendons showing along the bone like the dry twist of grapevine still corded on the stove-length of a hickory sapling" (p. 120). But soon we are reminded that wood can be sapped of its substance when a few pages later we read that York's wife wore a coat with "a scrap of fur at the collar which looked like some tattered growth of fungus feeding on old wood" (p. 124)—and when we realize that York was driven to suicide (appropriately, with a rope around his neck) when this wife with the parasitical collar cajoled him into giving up his farm for a hamburger stand. Once more, as in the title story, "old wood" is weathered and surrenders to "clawing vines."

We have not, however, touched upon all the articulations wrought by the imprint of Seth's father's heel on the context of the surrounding stories. It was the lieutenant's "near leg, the left leg," that Seth Sykes fatally touched in the parallel, embedded episode of "The Circus in the Attic," and it is to another left leg that our attention is drawn in the main narrative of that story—Bolton Lovehart's father's, which carries embedded within it a minnie ball "the size and shape of a man's thumb-tip" that had "flung him from his horse late in the afternoon of the Battle of Franklin" and now insistently throbs in the night, keeping him awake for hours (pp. 17–18). That the bullet is comparable to a man's thumb, that it struck him in the left leg, and that he was on a horse at the time are details that ought to throb in our memory and remind us of what transpired between Seth Sykes and the Union officer. But that memory, once acknowledged, still won't let us rest, for it poses a question that the story can't answer: Why should the Union lieutenant have anything in common with Confederate Major Simon Lovehart?

"Blackberry Winter" may provide an answer, for it takes these two incidents from the story that precedes it, blends them together, and gives them what looks like a happier ending. But just how positive that outcome is is not clear: Is the Seth of the first story indeed transformed into the Seth of the second, and are the horsemen—the lieutenant and the boy protagonist's father—of "Circus" changed into the boy protagonist's mounted father of "Blackberry Winter"? Are the filial trust and paternal reassurance of the second story undercut by the insistent memory of what happened in the first? Have we come close, in our discovery of such a resolution, to touching upon an underlying issue in Warren's fiction that would controvert the joy of that discovery?

Let us remember that precisely the reason Seth was approaching his father with some trepidation is that he feared his anger, and that that fear and that possible anger had something to do with feet: "Then I looked up and tried to read his face, to see if he was angry about my being barefoot." When the story began, to go shoeless was the narrator's overwhelming desire:

> I was standing on the hearth, almost into the chimney, hunched over the fire, working my bare toes slowly on the warm stone. I relished the heat which made the skin of my bare legs warp and creep and tingle, even as I called to my mother, who was somewhere back in the dining room or kitchen, and said: "But it's June, I don't have to put them on!" (p. 63).

It may be June, but it's also blackberry winter, or so his mother says. Seth gives us, if not his mother, a very specific reason for wanting to go barefoot:

> You do not understand that voice from back in the kitchen which says that you cannot go barefoot outdoors and run to see what has happened and rub your feet over the wet shivery grass and make the perfect mark of your foot in the smooth, creamy, red mud and then muse upon it as though you had suddenly come upon that single mark on the glistening auroral beach of the world. You have never seen a beach, but you have read the book and how the footprint was there. (p. 64).

If Bolton Lovehart's circus was a kind of writing, all the more so is Seth's footprint, which as soon as he makes it assumes writing's characteristic quality of appearing to have been made by someone else. Seth is in fact rehearsing what will happen in the book in which his story appears, for when we see this barefoot print again (and the mud has dried to dust) it will appear as the mark of another, indeed of a black companion like the Friday Seth was thinking of: "Alec devoted his attention to making elaborate and perfect footprints in which the dust outlined the creases of the skin and stood up beautifully in the spaces between his toes" (p. 216). Alec is Little Thomas's black playmate in "Prime Leaf," the last story in the collection, a role

analogous to that of Little Jebb in "Blackberry Winter." A measure of
the precision and subtlety of the structural connections underlying the
Circus stories is a coincidence of names like the one of the two Seths
that links Alec to Little Jebb through another Alec who bears a
resemblance of his own to Little Jebb: "A Christian Education"
concludes with a note on the fate of Silas Nabb's younger brother, who
did not have to undergo Silas's "Christian education" (with its injunc-
tion to turn the other cheek), whose name was Alec, and who did not
turn out much better. "Alec turned out to be a terror. . . . When he
was about twenty-two he got in a row and shot a man with a .38. The
man died. Alec is over in Nashville in the pen now, and I guess he'll
be there a good long time" (p. 142). "Blackberry Winter" closes with a
similar epilogue: "As for Little Jebb, he grew up to be a mean and ficey
Negro. He killed another Negro in a fight and got sent to the
penitentiary, where he is yet, the last I heard tell" (p. 86). *Circus* works
like the kind of poetry Warren was talking about when he wrote in
"Pure and Impure Poetry" that "poetry does not inhere in any
particular element but depends upon the set of relationships, the
structure, which we call the poem."[15] Read by itself, "A Christian
Education" does not yield up the meaning it can offer when read nearly
midway between "Blackberry Winter" and "Prime Leaf." And neither
do the other two. Put another way, the *Circus* stories are only stories
when read singly, some of them as clumsy, contrived, awkward or
slight as anyone has said them to be (Casper complains that the
characters in "Education" are "eccentric" and the narrative line "off
center":[16] This is precisely the point, that the story's center of gravity
cannot be calculated without taking into account the wider context);
but when read as elements in a set of relationships, and in a structure,
they come close to fulfilling Warren's own definition of a poem.

To the extent that *The Circus in the Attic* is a poem, the footprint Seth
makes and then imagines he discovered is the same footprint we
discover in "Prime Leaf," for the underlying argument of this poem is
the story of those reappearing elements whose comings and goings we
have been paying attention to here. To their list should be added the
hearth Seth stands on as he responds to his mother's voice from another
room in the house; it reappears in "Testament of Flood," in which the
boy protagonist "crouched on the tile hearth and stared at the
disintegrating embers. He heard his mother's voice from the next
room" (p. 166). And its re-emergence in "Prime Leaf" is joined by
some other notable images from "Blackberry Winter"—a father on

horseback, a son who tries, as Seth had, to read his father's thoughts by reading his impassive face: As Big Thomas, both a father (to Little Thomas) and a son (to Joe Hardin), fixed his gaze on the family hearth, "his eyes stared into the depth of the embers like those of a man who sees something he desires but may not have. Then his wife laughed" (p. 247). One thing he desires but cannot easily obtain—seems to possess—is his wife's admiration and love.

> "You and Papa are mighty different. I don't know which one of you I like the best."
> "I know which one. It's him."
> "Maybe so, maybe you're right." And then she caught sight of her husband's face. "Why, Thomas! . . . I do believe you're jealous of your own father. You ought to be spanked like Tommy."
> He turned and stared directly at her with the same look in his eyes as when he had been staring into the center of the fire. (pp. 247–248)

The immediately preceding story, "The Unvexed Isles," might have alerted us to expect a scene of jealousy around a fireplace. There, Professor Dalrymple had reason to be suspicious, for he happened to notice that the cigarette his student guest had laid on the ashtray was stained with lipstick. The young man had "a kind of aimless vitality that seemed to make the fire burn up brighter and the bulbs behind their parchment shades glow with more assurance" (p. 200). Now in the brief "Testament of Flood," Steve Adams, the son we might presume of the Thomas Adams who unsuccessfully courted Elsie Barton in the immediately preceding story ("The Love of Elsie Barton") had been consumed with desire for Elsie's daughter, Helen Beaumont, thinking about her incessantly as they both sat in the schoolroom; stoking his desire for that which he could not have, he stared at the "swollen bulb of the stove" glowing with heat. "At noon recess the older girls sat near the stove to eat their lunches. Heat flushed their cheeks and their voices harbored a subdued excitement" (p. 165). In "The Love of Elsie Barton," after Elsie threw over Thomas Adams for Benjamin Beaumont, she would sit, as her girl friends teased her about him, "with a secret, sweet thought in her head, like the piece of candy a child holds on its tongue and secretly sucks . . . and a little spot of color would glow in either of her cheeks" (p. 153). Both of these girlish glows and groupings reaffirm what we may have already seen in the swollen bulb of the stove that glowed like their cheeks (from "red" to "tint of rose" as it cooled at the end of the schoolday [p. 166]), the sexuality of their "subdued excitement" (p. 165) and his. Thus, in "The Unvexed Isles," the linkage of fire and glowing bulbs in the observation on the effects of Phil Alburt's "aimless vitality" is no accident. All of this comes to a head in a remarkable scene involving the professor, the professor's wife, Alburt, and the fireplace:

> Alice Dalrymple gave her gaze to the fire, where flames scrolled ornamentally upward to the black chimney throat. The brass dogs gleamed, the hearth was swept to a sharp border, the flames sprouted upward like flowers from an accurate parterre. . . . Alice Dalrymple held her head at right angles to the young man's chair; her profile was clean and delicate, with a careful dyspeptic beauty. The young man himself was looking into the fire. (p. 203)

A closer look focuses on Alice's throat: *"When she laughs now she holds her head up so the skin won't sag in her neck. Craning her neck like that, she looks like a cigarette advertisement"* (p. 205). Her throat invites a cigarette, or nourishes the thought of a cigarette, as the "black chimney throat" of the fireplace draws the flame. The right angles of her pose, the clean look of her profile, and the "accurate modulation" of her laugh (p. 205) recall, respectively, the "sharp border" and clean-swept look of the hearth and its appearance of being an "accurate" bed for sprouting flames. If Alice is the hearth, Phil with his "aimless vitality" supplies the flame—as does the elder Mr. Hardin in "Prime Leaf" when he "got down to his knees and began to blow Edith's remnant of coals back to flame" (p. 267). And it is with reason that the coals bear her name, for Edith is as closely connected to that hearth as Alice was to hers. When she sits at her fireplace, a sense of order prevails in the surrounding chaos, as if things were now in their right places; her robe falls to the hearth and almost makes her one with those stones: "She . . . wore a blue flannel robe which dropped loosely from her shoulders to the stone of the hearth and crumpled there to give a strange impression of arrangement in the cold disorder of the room" (p. 264).

The drama of the struggle between father and son in "Prime Leaf" is played out on the stage of that hearth. What is at issue is participation in or denunciation of the tobacco farmers' association at the moment of its strategic shift from boycott to terror. The elder Mr. Hardin had resigned from the board of directors to protest this new direction and said he would leave the association itself the first time it burned a barn. The day the younger Mr. Hardin stared at his wife the way he stared at the fire, with the eyes of a man who sees something he desires but may not have, and the day his wife accused him of being jealous of his own father, Joe Hardin arrived with the evening paper and its news of the nightriders' burning three barns. The newspaper was in his pocket when he came in to sit by the fire opposite his son, "propped his stick against the stonework of the fireplace, and began filling his pipe." After the first few puffs, he took out the paper and handed it to his son, who stared at it intently as he had gazed at the fire, and when he turned a page, "hunting the rest of the story, the paper crackled sharply in the silence, like a new-lit log at night." Thomas holds fire in his hands, in the smile that makes the paper sound like a crackling log and in the incendiary news it brings—and perhaps in another sense as well, if we pay attention to what happens in the background as he reads: "His father watched him; he still held the pipe fixed between his teeth while he watched, but no more puffs of smoke came from it" (p. 251). Some kind of fire has passed from father to son, or so at least the son would hope, if, as one might suspect, his principal motivation is to possess the erotic fire that would command his wife's allegiance and desire, to steal it away from his father. How appropriate it is then that when he finished the article and began to argue with his father about the association he should get up from the stool and step "to the center of the hearth." The hearth is more than high ground; it is the prize for which the battle is fought. Simply to occupy it gives Thomas an immediate apparent advantage over his father: "His father, sitting in the chair with the newspaper on his lap, looked very small before him" (p. 252). But Thomas's moral disadvantage is very real: His father had been the first to oppose the oppression of the tobacco buyers by joining the association, and had persuaded his son to come along. Now it appears that it is just as heroic to oppose the oppression of the association's terrorist tactics, and the father has been the first to make a moral point of leaving. Standing on the hearth, the younger Hardin accuses his father of endangering the family farm by having made a mistake he can't correct now:

> "You helped start this association. You got us in it and you got a lot of other people in it. You've started something and you can't stop it, so you're getting out. You made your mistake when you got off the

board. Papa, you're on horseback now, you're on horseback, and it's
a wild piece of horseflesh." (p. 253)

The image he adopts is curious, and perhaps premonitory, for after
much discussion and Thomas's eventual turnabout decision to leave
the association with his father and sell out their crop together, he will
try, fatally, another heroic tack: Their own barn is burned that night
and, too late to prevent that disaster or even for the act to be justified
as self-defense, Thomas will go out with a gun and shoot a nightrider
off his horse. When he returns to the house to tell his father what he
has done and Mr. Hardin begins to telephone to find out who it is that
has been hurt, Thomas's victorious pose on the hearth takes on a look
of sexual triumph: "Thomas stood on the hearth, rigidly erect, and
never shifted his eyes from his father's face. The face was inscrutable
and tired" (p. 272).

If we have the feeling that in aiming at the nightrider he was also
aiming at his father, it may be not only because he had just accused his
father of being on horseback but also because at that moment he was
re-enacting a sequence of events we have seen enacted before in "The
Circus in the Attic" and in "Blackberry Winter": The outcome was
very different, but when Seth approached his father on horseback, and
came almost close enough to touch his heel, he had "tried to read his
face," that "impassive" paternal face. Likewise Thomas never shifted
his eyes from his father's "inscrutable" face. The persistent focus on
the leg of a man on horseback, already noted in "Circus" and
"Blackberry Winter," continues here, in "Prime Leaf," for we are twice
given some very specific information concerning the legs of the man
Thomas shot. It was Mr. Hopkins, whose "thick, booted legs almost
gave the look of deformity" (p. 240; and earlier: "His thick legs were
ridiculously short, and the boots which he wore almost gave the look of
a deformity" [p. 228]).

Fathers are not alone in their inscrutability in Warren's fiction;
mothers are indecipherable because of what they say. Bolton Lovehart's mother uttered those passionate cries that could be misread as
anguish at the death of her husband; only time could show they were
really cries of triumph. But her cries are not always as susceptible of
interpretation as that, for when Bolton later tried to persuade her to see
a specialist for her heart condition "she uttered again the wild,
indecipherable, ambiguous, untranslatable cries which she had uttered
by the fallen body of Simon Lovehart" (p. 34). They are made more

difficult to decipher by the narrator's claim that they are the same cries, for the situation is entirely different: How could they be cries either of anguish or of triumph? More likely than either is that they articulate nothing but the fact of their articulation, sounds uttered merely in order to keep Bolton off balance, to convince him of her otherness and of his inability ever to interpret her. And if their second articulation is made more difficult to interpret by a changed context, what are we to make of the fact that they appear on yet another occasion divorced not only from that context but from that speaker as well? When Bolton tries to steal a kiss from Sara Darter, she, too, we recall, "screamed at him with furious words which he could not interpret" (p. 32). If what the narrator says is true about having to wait until the flesh of the passion has withered away to interpret such articulations, to wait until instead of hearing them we see with scrutinizing eyes the logical articulation of fact with fact, then perhaps not only the passion but the speaker too is unimportant. Perhaps it does not matter so much that Bolton's mother or that Sara Darter uttered those cries as it does that they were uttered at all, that Bolton finds himself in the position of being unable to interpret them—the same Bolton Lovehart who found himself unable to write the history of his country and constructed a soft pine circus instead.

Professor Dalrymple finds himself in a similar position of remoteness from the world in "The Unvexed Isles":

> As he turned about and traversed the excessive distance across the blue carpet, he felt that all these objects accumulated around him—table, chair, chair, blue carpet, rug, lamp—were unfamiliar to him, and now for the first time might, if he so chose, be construed in their unique and rich unities. After he had adjusted the tray, with special care, on the stand, he gave to its obscure design a lingering and analytic regard. Lingering . . . as if his attention to the intricacies of the design might postpone the need to inspect those people whose voices, somewhat remotely, impinged upon him. (p. 201)

If Bolton found a distraction in objects of his own making, Dalrymple is distracted by everyday, pre-existent objects that for others, and for himself before this moment, were mere background detail of no importance. Suddenly they demand his attention, and in their unfamiliarity, their opacity, acquire a rich existence of their own. We may

be so accustomed to valuing engagement with the "real world" that
when such a disengagement as Bolton or Dalrymple choose appears
before us in a work of fiction we too easily assume that we are being
exhorted to beware their evil example. Yet what Dalrymple does is
precisely what Warren's collection of stories encourages us to do and
what we have done in these pages, to read these narratives less for their
passion than for their connection of fact with fact, for the way they
succeed in making such homely things as lamps, stoves, hearths,
shoes, legs and limps uncannily unfamiliar. There is a certain remoteness attached to this critical activity that has more to do with
Dalrymple's discovery of the aesthetics of everyday objects and the
intricacies of their design than it does with the kind of vicarious desire
for intervention that we might nevertheless have wished that the
Professor had exercised. But he does not intervene in the drama or
farce that he thinks is being played out between his wife and the
student guest, and, serene to the end, lingers downstairs alone after
she has gone up to bed. "Somewhere on the upper floor a light burned,
splaying shadow and angular patches of illumination into the lower
section like a gigantic, ghostly pack of cards" (p. 209). This light from
the upper reaches of the house illumines more than Professor Dalrymple realizes, for it is the ghost of an image from the first page of the
immediately preceding story, "The Life and Work of Professor Roy
Millen"—likewise about a professor and a student of whom he had
reason to be jealous; Millen recalls "long tranquil evenings at the
bridge table with the light glinting subduedly on the exciting and rich
designs of the royal cards" (p. 190). Dalrymple was struck by the rich
unities and intricate design of what he saw in the household furnishings; we have reason to be struck by the rich unity of these two
passages, and to suspect an underlying intricacy of design. By design or
not, the presence of this image in two so similar and contiguous stories
should be cause for reflection. Yet it is not exactly the same image, for
the playing cards at the beginning of the first of these two stories are
real, their designs revealed by the glinting light, while their counter-
parts on the next-to-last page of the second are imaginary, brought into
existence only by a trick of the light from upstairs, gigantic ghost cards
occupying the space that had earlier been inhabited by those everyday
furnishings that had first attracted Dalrymple's gaze. Perhaps their
significance is that difference, a movement of greater remoteness from
the world that Dalrymple was pursuing when he was distracted from
the impinging voices by what he could construe of the design that

surrounded him. Like Bolton's circus constructions, the second set of cards is no longer something merely perceived, like the furniture, but Dalrymple's own creation, a trick of the light that wouldn't have worked without his participation. And like the circus in the attic, these cards are playthings, cardboard surfaces as subject to playful manipulation as the wooden tigers and trapeze artists of Bolton's upstairs menagerie. Representative as they are of the kind of double images Warren's *Circus* provides, where so much happens more than once, in a different context, for different reasons, and with different actors, the second pack of cards in particular seems especially indicative of the kind of reading this book (as opposed to its stories separately considered) invites.

Notes

1. "Prototype, Byblow and Reconception: Notes on the Relation of Warren's *The Circus in the Attic* to His Novels and Poetry," *Mississippi Quarterly*, 33 (Winter 1979–80), 3

2. *Robert Penn Warren: The Dark and Bloody Ground* (Seattle: Univ of Washington Press, 1960), p. 95.

3. Casper, p. 95.

4. *The Achievement of Robert Penn Warren* (Baton Rouge: Louisiana State Univ Press, 1981), pp. 15, 162.

5. *Robert Penn Warren*, rev. ed. (Boston: Twayne Publishers, 1981), p. 83.

6. Ruth Fisher, "A Conversation with Robert Penn Warren," *Four Quarters*, 21 (May 1972), 9.

7. "An Interview with Robert Penn Warren and Eleanor Clark," *The New England Review*, 1 (Fall 1978), 65.

8. Robert Penn Warren, *The Circus in the Attic and Other Stories* (New York: Harcourt Brace, 1947), p. 28. Further references to this work will appear parenthetically in the text.

9. See Casper.

10. Marshall Walker, *Robert Penn Warren: A Vision Earned* (Edinburgh: Paul Harris, 1979), p. 82.

11. Walker, p. 83.

12. James A. Grimshaw, *Robert Penn Warren: A Descriptive Bibliography, 1922–79* (Charlottesville: Univ Press of Virginia, 1981), pp. 228–230.

13. That they now have any order at all is new, for the stories never appeared together before. There is no single earlier order because the sequence of their appearance in various magazines and anthologies from 1931 to 1947 does not coincide with the order in which Warren wrote them. Though we do not know in exactly what order he did write them, we do know, for

example, that "Testament of Flood" and "The Love of Elsie Barton: A Chronicle," which first appeared in print in 1935 and 1946 respectively, were originally intended to appear together in chapters 2 through 4 of the untitled, uncompleted and unpublished novel Warren wrote in 1933–34.

14. As it happens, Seth's counterpart in the other story, the unfortunate Sykes, appears only in the version printed in the book, for the shorter version of "Circus" in the September 1947 issue of *Cosmopolitan* omits about 4,000 words (18%) of the text, including the entire Seth Sykes episode. It is less likely that the Sykes anecdote was added to the book version than restored there, for the magazine text repeats the story's later mention of the Sykes monument (*Cosmopolitan*, p. 83; *Circus*, p. 42) in a way that really makes no sense (since it assumes an acquaintance with Sykes that the reader could not have had) and cannot be accounted for except as a slip on the part of whoever—editor or author—shortened the story to make it conform to magazine length.

15. *Selected Essays* (New York: Random House, 1958), p. 26.

16. Casper, p. 96.

Chronology

1905   Born in Guthrie, Kentucky, 24 April; first child of Robert Franklin and Anna Ruth Penn Warren.

1921   Graduates from Clarksville (Tennessee) High School; enters Vanderbilt University.

1923–1925   Active in Nashville "Fugitive Group."

1925   Graduates from Vanderbilt University

1925–1927   Graduate student at University of California (M.A. 1927).

1927–1928   Graduate student at Yale University.

1928–1930   Rhodes Scholar, Oxford (B.Litt., 1930).

1929   *John Brown: The Making of a Martyr* (Biography).

1930   Assistant professor of English, Southwestern College, Memphis; marries Emma Brescia.

1931   "Prime Leaf" (Novella).

1931–1934   Assistant professor of English, Vanderbilt University.

1934–1942   Assistant professor (to 1936) and then associate professor of English, Louisiana State University.

1935   *Thirty-Six Poems*; founds the *Southern Review* with Cleanth Brooks.

1936   *An Approach to Literature* (Textbook).

1938   *Understanding Poetry* (Textbook).

1939   *Night Rider* (Novel) ; awarded first Guggenheim Fellowship.

1942   *Eleven Poems on the Same Theme*; professor of English, University of Minnesota, Minneapolis.

1943   *At Heaven's Gate* (Novel) ; *Understanding Fiction* (Textbook).

1944   *Selected Poems, 1923–1943*; holds Chair of Poetry, Library of Congress.

1946   *All the King's Men* (Novel, Pulitzer Prize and National Book Award); "Blackberry Winter" (Short story); "The Rime of the Ancient Manner" (Critical Essay).

1947   Awarded second Guggenheim Fellowship; *The Circus in the Attic and Other Stories.*

1949   Motion picture of *All the King's Men*; receives Robert Meltzer Award, from the Screen Writer's Guild, for his novel.

1950   *World Enough and Time* (Novel); Professor of drama at Yale University (until 1956); *Modern Rhetoric* (Textbook).

1951   Divorces Emma Brescia Warren.

1952   Marries Eleanor Clark; elected to American Philosophical Society.

1953   *Brother to Dragons: A Tale in Verse and Voices.*

1954   Daughter, Rosanna, born.

1955   *Band of Angels* (Novel).

1956   Son, Gabriel, born; *Segregation: The Inner Conflict in the South.*

1957   *Promises: Poems 1954–1956* (Pulitzer Prize, National Book Award, Edna St. Vincent Millay Prize of Poetry Society of America).

1958   *Selected Essays.*

1959   *The Cave* (Novel); elected to the American Academy of Arts and Letters.

1960   *You, Emperors, and Others: Poems 1957–1960*; *All the King's Men* (Play).

1961   *Wilderness* (Novel): *The Legacy of the Civil War*; professor of English, Yale University (until 1973).

1964   *Flood: A Romance of Our Time* (Novel).

1965   *Who Speaks for the Negro?*

1966   *Selected Poems: New and Old: 1923–1966*; awarded Bollingen Prize in Poetry.

1968   *Incarnations: Poems 1966-1968.*

1969   *Audubon: A Vision* (Narrative Poem); National Medal for Literature; Van Wyck Brooks Award.

1970 *Selected Poems of Herman Melville: A Reader's Edition.*

1971 *Meet Me in the Green Glen* (Novel); *Homage to Theodore Dreiser on The Centennial of His Birth*; *John Greenleaf Whittier's Poetry: An Appraisal and a Selection.*

1973 *American Literature: The Makers and the Making* (Textbook).

1974 *Or Else—Poem/Poems 1968–1974*; National Foundation for the Humanities Lectureship.

1975 *Democracy and Poetry*; Elected to American Academy of Arts and Sciences and (receives its Emerson-Thoreau Award).

1976 *Selected Poems 1923–1975*; Copernicus Prize for Poetry from the Academy of American Poets.

1977 *A Place to Come To* (Novel) ; Harriet Monroe Prize for Poetry.

1978 *Now and Then: Poems 1976–1978* (Pulitzer Prize).

1979 *Brother to Dragons: A Tale in Verse and Voices: A New Version.*

1980 *Jefferson Davis Gets His Citizenship Back*; *Being Here: Poetry 1977–1980.*

1981 *Rumor Verified: Poems 1979–1980*; Awarded MacArthur Fellowship.

1983 *Chief Joseph of the Nez Perce* (Narrative Poem).

1985 *Altitudes and Extensions: Poems 1980–1984*; *New and Selected Poems: 1923–1985.*

1986 Named Poet Laureate of the United States.

1988 *Portrait of a Father* (Reminiscence).

1989 *New and Selected Essays; dies 15 September at Stratton, Vermont.*

Selected Bibliography

Primary Works

Individual Stories (Chronological)

Blackberry Winter. Cummington, Mass.: Cummington Press, 1946.
"A Christian Education." *Mademoiselle*, January 1945, pp. 96–97, 155–57.
"Christmas Gift." *Virginia Quarterly Review* 13 (Winter 1937): 73–85.
"The Circus in the Attic." *Cosmopolitan*, September 1947, pp. 67–70, 73–74, 76, 78, 80, 83–84, 86, 88.
"The Confession of Brother Grimes." *New English Review*, 12 (June 1946):561–63.
"Her Own People." *Virginia Quarterly Review* 11 (April 1935):289–304.
"Goodwood Comes Back," *Southern Review* 6 (Winter 1941):526–36.
"Invitation to a Dance." *Today's Woman*, February 1949, pp. 45, 88.
"The Life and Work of Professor Roy Millen." *Mademoiselle*, February 1943, pp. 145–49.
"The Love of Elsie Barton: A Chronicle." *Mademoiselle*, December 1946, pp. 161, 282–90.
"The Patented Gate and the Mean Hamburger." *Mademoiselle*, January 1947. pp. 188–89, 242–43, 245–46.
"Prime Leaf." *American Caravan* 4 (1931): 3–61.
"Testament of Flood." *Magazine* 2 (March–April 1935): 230-34.
"The Unvexed Isles." *Magazine* 2 (July–August 1934); 1–10.
"When the Light Gets Green." *Southern Review* 1 (Spring 1936): 799–806.

Short Fiction Collection

The Circus in the Attic and Other Stories. New York: Harcourt, Brace, 1947.

Non-fiction

American Literature: The Makers and the Making, 2 vols., Cleanth Books, R.W.B. Lewis, and Robert Penn Warren, eds. (New York: St. Martin's Press, 1973).
Democracy and Poetry. Cambridge: Harvard University Press, 1975.
Homage to Theodore Dreiser on the Centennial of His Birth. New York: Random House, 1971.

Jefferson Davis Gets His Citizenship Back. Lexington: University Press of Kentucky, 1980.

John Brown: The Making of a Martyr. New York: Payson and Clarke, 1929.

John Greenleaf Whittier's Poetry: An Appraisal and a Selection. Minneapolis: University of Minnesota Press, 1971.

The Legacy of the Civil War: Meditations on the Centennial. New York: Random House, 1961.

New and Selected Essays. New York: Random House, 1989.

Portrait of a Father. Lexington: University Press of Kentucky, 1988.

Segregation: The Inner Conflict in the South. New York: Random House, 1956.

Selected Essays. New York: Random House, 1958.

Selected Poems of Herman Melville: A Reader's Edition. New York: Random House, 1970.

Who Speaks for the Negro? New York: Random House, 1965.

Fiction

All the King's Men. New York: Harcourt, Brace and Company, 1946. New York: Random House, Modern Library, 1953.

At Heaven's Gate. New York: Harcourt, Brace and Company, 1943.

Band of Angels. New York: Random House, 1955.

The Cave. New York: Random House, 1959.

Flood: A Romance of Our Time. New York: Random House, 1964.

Meet Me in the Green Glen. New York: Random House, 1971.

Night Rider. Boston: Houghton Mifflin and Company, 1939.

A Place to Come To. New York: Random House, 1977.

Wilderness: A Tale of the Civil War. New York: Random House, 1961.

World Enough and Time: A Romantic Novel. New York: Random House, 1950.

Play

All the King's Men: A Play. New York: Random House, 1960.

Poetry

Altitudes and Extensions: Poems 1980–1984. New York: Random House, 1985.

Audubon: A Vision. New York: Random House, 1971.

Being Here: Poetry 1979–1980. New York: Random House, 1980.

Brother to Dragons: A Tale in Verse and Voices. New York: Random House, 1953. Rev. ed. *Brother to Dragons: A Tale in Verse and Voices: A New Version.* New York: Random House, 1979.

Chief Joseph of the Nez Perce. New York: Random House, 1983.

Eleven Poems on the Same Theme. Norfolk, Conn.: New Directions, 1942.

Incarnations: Poems 1966–1968. New York: Random House, 1968.

New and Selected Poems: 1923–1985. New York: Random House, 1985.

Now and Then: Poems 1976–1978. New York: Random House, 1978.

Or Else—Poem/Poems 1968–1974. New York: Random House, 1974.

Promises: Poems 1954–1956. New York: Random House, 1957.

Rumor Verified: Poems 1979–1980. New York: Random House, 1981.

Selected Poems, 1923–1943. New York: Harcourt, Brace and Company, 1944.

Selected Poems: New and Old, 1923–1966. New York: Random House, 1966.

Selected Poems: 1923–1975. New York: Random House, 1976.

Thirty-Six Poems. New York: Alcestis Press, 1935.

You, Emperors, and Others: Poems 1957–1960. New York: Random House, 1960.

Secondary Works

Books

Bohner, Charles. *Robert Penn Warren: Revised Edition*. Boston: Twayne, 1981.

Burt, John. *Robert Penn Warren and American Idealism*. New Haven: Yale University Press, 1988.

Casper, Leonard. *Robert Penn Warren: The Dark and Bloody Ground*. Seattle: University of Washington Press, 1960.

Justus, James H. *The Achievement of Robert Penn Warren*. Baton Rouge: Louisiana State University Press, 1981.

Runyon, Randolph Paul. *The Taciturn Text: The Fiction of Robert Penn Warren*. Columbus: Ohio State University Press, 1990.

Snipes, Katherine. *Robert Penn Warren*. New York: Frederick Ungar, 1983.

Walker, Marshall. *Robert Penn Warren: A Vision Earned*. New York: Barnes and Noble, 1979.

Watkins, Floyd. *Then and Now: The Personal Past in the Poetry of Robert Penn Warren*. Lexington: University Press of Kentucky, 1982.

West, Paul. *Robert Penn Warren*. Minneapolis: University of Minnesota Press, 1964.

Articles

Boone, Joy Bale. "A Circus at the Top." *Louisville Courier-Journal Magazine*, 4 June 1978, pp. 10–15.

Fiedler, Leslie. "The Fate of the Novel." *Kenyon Review* 10 (1948): 519–27.

Fridy, Will. "The Author and the Ballplayer: An Imprint of Memory in the Writings of Robert Penn Warren." *Mississippi Quarterly* 44 (1991): 159–66.

Grubbs, Morris. "Conflict and Synthesis in Robert Warren's 'Blackberry Winter.'" *Western Kentucky University Student Honors Research Bulletin* (1989–90): 22–25.

O'Connor, William Van. "Robert Penn Warren's Short Fiction." *Western Review* 12 (1948): 180–87.

Runyon, Randolph. "The View from the Attic: Robert Penn Warren's *Circus Stories*." *Mississippi Quarterly* 38 (1985): 119–35.

Shepherd, Allen G. "Prototype, Byblow and Reconception: Notes on the Relation of Warren's *The Circus in the Attic* to His Novels and Poetry." *Mississippi Quarterly* 33 (1979): 3–17.

Shepherd, Allen G. "Robert Penn Warren's 'Prime Leaf' as Prototype of *Night Rider*." *Studies in Short Fiction* 7 (1970): 469–71.

Weathers, Winston. "'Blackberry Winter' and the Use of Archetypes." *Studies in Short Fiction* 1 (1963): 45–51.

Wilhelm, Albert E. "Images of Initiation in Robert Penn Warren's 'Blackberry Winter.'" *Studies in Short Fiction* 17 (1980) : 343–45.

Theory and Criticism of the Short Story

Ingram, Forrest L. *Representative Short Story Cycles of the Twentieth Century: Studies in a Literary Genre.* The Hague: Mouton Press, 1971.

Mann, Susan Garland. *The Short Story Cycle.* Westport, Conn.: Greenwood Press, 1989.

May, Charles E. *Short Story Theories.* Athens: Ohio University Press, 1976.

Peden, William. *The American Short Story: Continuity and Change, 1940–1975.* 2d ed. Boston: Houghton Mifflin, 1975.

Stevick, Philip, ed. *The American Short Story, 1900-1945: A Critical History.* Boston: Twayne, 1984.

Voss, Arthur. *The American Short Story: A Critical Survey.* Norman: University of Oklahoma Press, 1973.

Weaver, Gordon, ed. *The American Short Story, 1945–1980: A Critical History.* Boston: Twayne, 1983.

West, Ray B., Jr. *The Short Story in America: 1900–1950.* Freeport, N.Y.: Books for Libraries Press, 1968.

Bibliography

Grimshaw, James A., Jr. *Robert Penn Warren: A Descriptive Bibliography, 1922–79.* Charlottesville: University Press of Virginia, 1981.

Index

The Author

Joseph R. Millichap received his doctorate from Notre Dame University. He is professor of English and head of the English Department at Western Kentucky University, as well as director of its Center for the Study of Robert Penn Warren. His publications include three books, a monograph, and over 50 articles on American literature and film, particularly the fiction of the Southern Renaissance.

The Editor

General Editor Gordon Weaver earned his B.A. in English at the University of Wisconsin-Milwaukee in 1961; his M.A. in English at the University of Illinois, where he studied as a Woodrow Wilson Fellow, in 1962: and his Ph.D. in English and creative writing at the University of Denver in 1970. He is author of several novels, including *Count a Lonely Cadence, Give Him A Stone, Circling Byzantium*, and, most recently, *The Eight Corners of the World* (1988). Many of his numerous short stories are collected in *The Entombed Man of Thule, Such Waltzing Was Not Easy, Getting Serious, Morality Play, A World Quite Round*, and *Men Who Would Be Good* (1991). Recognition of his fiction includes the St. Lawrence Award for Fiction (1973), two National Endowment for the Arts Fellowships (1974, 1989), and the O. Henry First Prize (1979). He edited *The American Short Story, 1945–1980: A Critical History*, and is currently editor of *Cimarron Review*. He is professor of English at Oklahoma State University and serves as an adjunct member of the faculty of the Vermont College Master of Fine Arts in Writing Program. Married, and the father of three daughters, he lives in Stillwater, Oklahoma.